Bronx Masquerade

Bronx Masquerade

by Nikki Grimes

Dial Books
NEW YORK

Published by Dial Books
A division of Penguin Putnam Inc.
345 Hudson Street
New York, New York 10014

Copyright © 2002 by Nikki Grimes
All rights reserved
Designed by Nancy R. Leo-Kelly
Text set in Stempel Garamond
Printed in the U.S.A. on acid-free paper
3 5 7 9 10 8 6 4 2

Library of Congress Cataloging-in-Publication Data
Grimes, Nikki.
Bronx masquerade / by Nikki Grimes.
p.   cm.
Summary: While studying the Harlem Renaissance, students at a Bronx
high school read aloud poems they've written, revealing their
innermost thoughts and fears to their formerly clueless classmates.
ISBN 0-8037-2569-8
[1. Poetry—Fiction. 2. Identity—Fiction. 3. Ethnicity—Fiction.
4. Afro-Americans—Fiction. 5. High schools—Fiction.
6. Schools—Fiction. 7. Bronx (New York, N.Y.)—Fiction.]
I. Title.
PZ7.G88429 Br 2002   [Fic]—dc21   00-031701

Bronx Masquerade

Wesley "Bad Boy" Boone

I ain't particular about doing homework, you understand. My teachers practically faint whenever I turn something in. Matter of fact, I probably got the longest list of excuses for missing homework of anyone alive. Except for my homey Tyrone. He tries to act like he's not even interested in school, like there's no point in studying hard, or dreaming about tomorrow, or bothering to graduate. He's got his reasons. I keep on him about going to school, though, saying I need the company. Besides, I tell him, if he drops out and gets a J.O.B., he won't have any time to work on his songs. That always gets to him. Tyrone might convince everybody else that he's all through with dreaming, but I know he wants to be a big hip-hop star. He's just afraid he won't live long enough to do it. Me, I hardly ever think about checking out. I'm more worried about figuring what I want to do if I live.

Anyway, I haven't had to drag Tyrone off to school lately, or make excuses for not having my homework done, because I've been doing it. It's the Harlem Renaissance stuff that's got us both going.

We spent a month reading poetry from the Harlem Renaissance in our English class. Then Mr. Ward—that's our teacher—asked us to write an essay about it. Make sense to you? Me neither. I mean, what's the point of studying *poetry* and then writing *essays*? So I wrote a bunch of poems instead. They weren't too shabby, considering I'd only done a few rap pieces before. My favorite was about Langston Hughes. How was I to know Teach would ask me to read it out loud? But I did. Knees knocking like a skeleton on Halloween, embarrassment bleaching my black cheeks red, eyes stapled to the page in front of me. But I did it, I read my poem.

Guess what. Nobody laughed. In fact, everybody thought it was cool. By the time I got back to my seat, other kids were shouting out: "Mr. Ward, I got a poem too. Can I bring it in to read?"

Teach cocked his head to the side, like he was hearing something nobody else did.

"How many people here have poems they'd like to read?" he asked. Three hands shot up. Mr. Ward rubbed his chin for a minute. "Okay," he said. "Bring them with you tomorrow."

After class Teach came over to my desk. "Great poem," said Mr. Ward. "But I still expect to see an essay from you. I'll give you another week." So much for creative expression.

Long Live Langston

BY WESLEY BOONE

Trumpeter of Lenox and 7th
through Jesse B. Semple,
you simply celebrated
Blues and Be-bop
and being Black before
it was considered hip.
You dipped into
the muddy waters
of the Harlem River
and shouted "taste and see"
that we Black folk be good
at fanning hope
and stoking the fires
of dreams deferred.
You made sure
the world heard
about the beauty of
maple sugar children, and the
artfully tattooed backs of Black
sailors venturing out
to foreign places.

Your Sweet Flypaper of Life
led us past the Apollo and on
through 125th and all the other
Harlem streets you knew like
the black of your hand.
You were a pied-piper, brother man
with poetry as your flute.
It's my honor and pleasure to salute
You, a true Renaissance man
of Harlem.

Tyrone Bittings

School ain't nothin' but a joke. My moms don't want to hear that, but if it weren't for Wesley and my other homeys, I wouldn't even be here, aiight? These white folk talking 'bout some future, telling me I need to be planning for some future—like I got one! And Raynard agreeing, like he's smart enough to know. From what I hear, that boy can't hardly read! Anyway, it's them white folk that get me with this *future* mess. Like Steve, all hopped up about working on Broadway and telling me I should think about getting with it too. Asked me if I ever thought about writing plays. "Fool! What kinda question is that?" I said. He threw his hands up and backed off a few steps. "All I'm saying is, you're a walking drama, man. You got that down pat, so maybe you should think about putting it on paper." When that boy dyed his hair, I b'lieve some of that bleach must've seeped right into his brain. I grind my teeth and lower my voice. "Boy, get out my face," I tell him. He finally gets the message and splits. I'm ticked off that he even got me *thinking* about such nonsense as Broadway.

White folk! Who they think they kidding? They might as well go blow smoke up somebody else's you-know-what, 'cause a Black man's got no chance in this country. I be lucky if I make it to twenty-one with all these fools running round with AK-47s. Here I am one of the few kids I know whose daddy *didn't* skip out on him, and he didn't even make it to thirty. He was doing okay 'til he got blown away on a Saturday. Blam! Another statistic in a long line of drive-bys. Life is cold. Future? What I got is right now, right here, spending time with my homeys. Wish there was some future to talk about. I could use me some future.

I'm just about ready to sleep off the whole year when this teacher starts talking about poetry. And he rattles off a poem by some white guy named Dylan Thomas that sounds an awful lot like rap. Now, I know me some rap, and I start to thinking I should show Mr. Ward what rap is really all about. So I tell him I've got a poem I'd like to read. "Bring it on Friday," he says. "As a matter of fact, from now on, I'll leave time for poetry readings at the end of every month. We'll call them Open Mike Fridays." Next thing I know, I'm digging my old rap poems out of my dresser drawer and bringing them to school. I'm thinking it can't hurt to share them, even if there's no chance I'll ever get to be a songwriter. After all, it's the one thing I could see myself doing if there really was a future. And I'm thinking that maybe there could be if I wanted it bad enough. And all of a sudden, I realize I do.

Attendance

BY TYRONE BITTINGS

We are all here,
Leslie and Bad Boy, Lupe and Raul,
Here, here and here.
Dear Mr. Ward
with his wards and wardettes.
Let's have a show of hands today.
Is Porscha here? Is Diondra here?
Where oh where is Sheila?
It's me, Tyrone,
up here all alone
rapping into a microphone
'cause I've got something to say:
MTV is here, Mir and
morning space-walks are here,
terrorism is here
lurking at the bus stop.
Can't hop on the subway
without thinkin' of Tokyo—
we all know poison gas
does not discriminate.

It's too late to worry
about my innocence
since fear is here.
Why is it a weekend visit
to your local Mickey D's
may be deadly?
Why hasn't somebody
censored death?
Don't hold your breath waiting.
Still you can chill and celebrate
all that's great about life, like music
and the tick-tick-tick of time
which is equal parts yours and mine
to make of the world what we will.
But first, say no to coke, and smoke.
Say no to police brutality
and causing fatality.
Say no to race hate.
Don't underestimate
the power of love.
But most of all
take two poems
and call me
in the morning.

Chankara Troupe

I am not in the mood for Tyrone's sorry "Baby, gimme some loving" routine, so when I see him in the hall, I storm past as if he's not even there. Eventually, he'll figure out why.

I come to school sporting shades and a johnny-print across my left cheek, Johnny being the name of the idiot who smacked me last night. Naturally, Porscha is the first person who notices my new tattoo. She walks straight up to me and says, "You deserve better, girlfriend. And you know it." No hello. No how are you. Just: "You deserve better." Then she turns away and walks into the classroom. Typical Porscha. No nonsense. That's why we get along.

Then here comes Sheila Gamberoni. The minute she sees me, she demands to know the name of the guy who gave me my shiner, like she's gonna send her brothers after him or something. I keep his name to myself, just in case. She commences to call the guy everything but a child of God, which makes her feel better, I think, then gives me a hug and says she'll see me later. Sheila is a bit over the top with this sister act, as if she's trying to make up for being white, but she means well. I can do without some of the other girls who stare at me, though. I know they're just looking for something to talk about, so I rip off my sunglasses, let them get a better look. *Might as well stare all you want. This is the first and last time you'll ever see me like this.*

Of course, that's what they all say. Nobody knows that better than me. My sister's boyfriends have been beating on her for years. I made up my mind a long time ago, I'm not having none of that.

Last night I tried telling this to Johnny, who seems to be hard of hearing. He'd brought me home from a movie. He came in for a while, got comfortable since Mom was working overtime and we had the apartment to ourselves. We locked lips for a few minutes. Next thing I know, he's fingering my shirt buttons. I push him away, gently at first. "I think we better slow down," I say. "No, no," he says, voice all husky. "It's just getting good." This time, his hand shoots up my skirt. Bad move. I jump off the sofa like it's on fire. "Maybe it's time for you to go." He grabbed my skirt and tried pulling me back down, which is right about when I hauled off and smacked him. He leaped up and smacked me back.

My jaw dropped from shock, and I looked in his eyes and saw my sister's reflection.

I turned away, strode to the door, unlocked it, and held it open for him.

"I hope you enjoyed yourself," I said, "'cause that's the last time you'll ever lay a hand on me. Now get out!" He actually looked like he was studying on staying, so I stepped out into the hall and screamed at the top of my lungs, "I said get out!" Fearing trouble, he left.

Now I've got this ugly tattoo on my cheek. I thought about skipping school today, but I hate to miss English. Besides, the bruise is temporary and so is the pain. Still, I'd rather not have kids gawking at me all period, so I park myself in the back of the room and wait for Mr. Ward to call our English class to attention.

Mr. Ward is funny. Sometimes he asks us a question with no warning, and tells us to answer quick, without stopping to think about it. The truth is always right on the tip of your tongue, he says. It's the fabrications that take a lot of time. Yesterday he asked us: "What do you know?" Yesterday I said my name, but today would be different. Today I'd tell him a woman ain't no punching bag. That's what I know.

Bruised Love

BY CHANKARA TROUPE

A midnight thirst sent me
padding to the kitchen
for a jelly-jar of water
and an accidental run-in
with my sister.
She tiptoed in, late
and limping, her cheek
raw as red-brown meat.
I caught a quick glance
in the chilly glow
of the refrigerator
before she had
a chance to hide
the latest souvenir
her boyfriend gave her.
"I bruise easily"
is one of the lies
she sprinkles like sugar.
But I'm fifteen,
not brainless. Besides,
I knew the truth at ten.

"He'll never do it again,"
she swears.
But he will, because
she'll let him.
Now, me?
I've got no use
for lame excuses
or imitation love
that packs
a punch.

Tyrone

My pops used to hit my moms like that.

When I was little, I used to hide under my bed and cry, scared he was coming for me next. Damn, I ain't thought about that in years. How could you do that, Pops? I don't get it. Is that why he hung around? So he'd have somebody smaller than him to beat up on? I don't even want to go there. I'm just glad he finally stopped drinking and cleaned up his act before he checked out. It gave us a chance to have some good times together.

Chankara was the third one up today. Her stuff was so deep, nobody wanted to follow her. There weren't but two more people planning to read anyway, including me. We both decided to bag it 'til the next Open Mike.

Meanwhile, I'm going to be busy writing me a rap about dudes beatin' on women. I'll call it "Little Men," 'cause that's what they are.

Raul Ramirez

Lunch is a memory of indigestion. Chankara sat across from me in the cafeteria and I couldn't help staring at her. Her bruises are almost gone, but I can still see the shadows they left behind. If she was my *hermanita*, I'd squash the cockroach who messed her up like that. That's what I was thinking when I remembered it ain't nice to stare. So I ate too fast and got out of there before she could catch me.

Only twenty minutes 'til class starts, and Mr. Ward don't like it if I leave a mess on his desk, so that's eighteen minutes to paint, plus two more for cleaning up and washing the paintbrushes. If Raynard gets here early, he'll help. He always does, I don't know why. Tyrone's another story. He checks in early lots of times when I'm here, but he keeps his distance, usually. Once he came up behind me and watched over my shoulder while I worked. Made me kinda nervous, if you must know. The Ricans and the brothers don't always hit it off. Anyway, he stood there for the longest. Then he grunted and said, "You good, man, I'll give you that."

"Thanks," I said.

"You wasting your time, though. You know you ain't gonna make no money doing this."

"Maybe. Maybe not," I said. "But some things ain't about money."

"You tripping, man," said Tyrone. "Money is the alpha and omega. Ask anybody."

I just shrugged and gave him my *"No hablo ingles"* look, like I didn't get what he was talking about. It was the quickest way to end the conversation.

People just don't get it. Even if I never make a dime—which, by the way, ain't gonna happen—I'd still have to paint.

Don't get me wrong. Money is useful. I'm lucky Mr. Ward leaves brushes and watercolor paper for me to use, though I ain't gonna tell him that. It's none of his business I can't afford fancy brushes and watercolor paper at home. Anyway, it's good for him to help out the future Diego Rivera. He knows I'm the real deal. Didn't he come to me for advice on how to decorate the classroom? The paper frames were my idea. Good work belongs in a gallery, I told him. Especially if it's mine.

I never thought about writing poetry before, but Mr. Ward said he's going to start videotaping our Friday sessions. Guess who's going to be the first one in front of the camera. Of course, that means I have to write a poem, so I better get busy. Even if it's hard, I'll do it. I don't mind working hard. Whatever it takes, *¿entiendes?* Raul Ramirez, painter-poet. Yeah. I like the sound of that.

Someday I'll have a poetry reading and a one-man show at the Nuyorican Poets Cafe on the Lower East Side. I'll hand out tokens to all my friends so they got no excuse not to take the ride downtown, okay?

My brothers laugh at me just 'cause they've been in the world a little longer. They say I'm *loco en la cabeza,* that ain't no spic gonna be no big-time artist in America. "First off," I tell them, "I ain't no spic. And second, watch me."

Abuelita says my talent is as old as her bones. She says I got it, and my stubbornness, from her father. He never did nothing with his talent, though. I asked her why not. "*Porque la familia* could not eat paint," she said. So I will be the first painter in the family. That's fine with me.

I've been drawing pictures all my life. I used to make my sister model for me. I'd bribe her with whatever I could scrounge up from returning soda bottles to the grocery. Eventually, I got tired of digging through trash for bottles, and she got bored modeling. Now it's easier. My girlfriend sits for me. Every painter needs a model, right? Anyway, she knows if she's nice to me, one day I'll make her famous. Even if she's not nice, I'll probably paint her because she's beautiful.

I want to show the beauty of our people, that we are not all *banditos* like they show on TV, munching *cuchfritos* and sipping beer through chipped teeth. I will paint *los niños* scooping up laughter in the sunshine and splashing in the temporary pool of a fire hydrant. I will paint my cousins, turning the sidewalk into a dance floor when *salsa* or *la bamba* spills from the third-floor window. I will paint Mami, standing at the ironing board late in the evening, after a day of piecework in the factory, sweat pouring off her, steam rising from a pot in the background, me tugging at her skirt while she irons. I will paint the way she used to smile down at me, the love in her eyes saying "I only do this for you." Mami's beauty is better than a movie star's. It survives a kind of life where pamper is a noun, not a verb. I will capture that beauty on canvas, someday, when I am good enough.

For now, I draw in my sketchbook and paint portraits of myself for practice. But it's not so bad. I'm handsome, after all.

Zorro

BY RAUL RAMIREZ

Call me Zorro, all swash and buckle while the cam-
eras roll, cape swinging in the breeze, teeth show-
ing as expected. I lunge on cue, save the damsel in
distress. I understand my role. I've studied all
those scripts and comic books. I used to pose for
close-ups, knew how to dutifully disappear

when the script said:
"Fade to black." Then
I'd wait uncomfort-
ably between the lines
of my own story 'til
someone with skin like
milk yelled "Action!"
But I'm done. I'm too
old for comic heros. It's
time to lose the cape,

step off the page, except I think I'll keep the mask.
Why make it easy for you to choose whether I am
Zorro or el bandito when I am neither? Your cate-
gories are too confining. The fact is, you're more com-
fortable with myth than man. But I am here to help. First
off, put down your camera. Second, give me your hand.

Tyrone

Raul is on the money. You gotta make your own rules, Jack. That's the real 411. Forget who white folks think you are, 'cause they ain't got a *clue*.

That's some strong stuff Raul be writin'. That "Z" thing was cool too. He was working it.

Frankly, I didn't know Raul had it in him. Matter of fact, I didn't know he knew that much English!

Diondra Jordan

If only I was as bold as Raul. The other day, he left one of his paintings out on Mr. Ward's desk where anybody could see it. Which was the point. He sometimes works at Mr. Ward's desk during lunch. The wet paintbrushes sticking up out of the jar are always a sign that he's been at it again. So of course, anybody who glances over in that direction will be tempted to stop by and look.

This particular painting was rough, but anyone could tell it was Raul. A self-portrait. He'll probably hang it in class. Back in September, Mr. Ward covered two of the classroom walls with black construction paper and then scattered paper frames up and down the walls, each one a different size and color. Now half the room looks sort of like an art gallery, which was the idea. We're supposed to use the paper frames for our work. Whether we put up poems or photographs or even paintings is up to us, so long as the work is ours and we can tie it in with our study of the Harlem Renaissance. I guess Raul's self-portrait fits, since we've been talking a lot about identity. He'll probably put it up next to his poem. You should have seen him hang that thing. You'd think he was handling a million-dollar masterpiece the way he took his time placing it just so. If you look close, you can see the smudges where he erased a word or two and rewrote it. Mr. Ward must be in shock. He can never get Raul to rewrite a lick of homework or anything else. And don't even talk to him about checking his spelling! He'll launch into a tirade on you in a minute. "What?" he'll snap. "You think Puerto Ricans can't spell?" Forget it. Anyway, I dare you to find one misspelled word in that poem of his! Maybe it's a visual thing. Maybe he wants his poem to look as good as his self-portrait. And it is good.

I've never tried doing a self-portrait, but why not? I could maybe do one in charcoal. I like drawing faces in charcoal. I've been drawing since I can't remember when. Not that anyone here knows that, except Tanisha, and she found out by accident when she came to my house to study once and saw a couple of drawings hanging in my room. Mom loves my watercolors and she hung one in the living room, but it isn't signed. Nobody ever mentions it, especially not my father. He's not too wild about my art. Mostly, he's disappointed, first off that I wasn't born a boy, and second that I won't play ball like one. I'm six feet tall, almost as tall as he, and he figures the height is wasted on me since I don't share his dreams of me going to the WNBA. I keep telling him not to hold his breath.

I hate always being the tallest girl in school. Everybody expects me to play basketball, so they pick me for their team, throw me the ball, and wait for me to shoot. Big mistake. I fumble it every time. Then they have the nerve to get mad at me, like I did it on purpose! But basketball is not my game. I have no game. I'm an artist, like Raul. The difference is, I don't tell anybody. I refuse to give them new reasons to laugh at me. The Jolly Green Giant jokes are bad enough.

Yeah, it's definitely time to try a self-portrait. I think I'll paint myself in front of an easel. With a basketball jersey sticking up out of the trash. Then I could hang it in Mr. Ward's class. See if anybody notices.

If

BY DIONDRA JORDAN

If I stood on tiptoe
reached up and sculpted
mountains from clouds
would you laugh out loud?

If I dipped my brush in starlight
painted a ribbon of night
on your windowsill
would you still laugh?

If I drew you adrift
in a pen and ink sea
in a raging storm
would you laugh at me?

If I planted watercolor roses
in your garden
would you laugh then?
Or would you breathe deep
to sample their scent?
I wonder.

Tyrone

If the sista read any faster, I'd be looking for her Supergirl cape. Talk about nervous! Diondra's hands were shaking the whole time she was holding that poem. She sure spooks easy for somebody so tall.

"Yo!" I said. "Take a deep breath. Ain't nobody going to hurt you here." She smiled a little and tried to slow down. But I swear that girl burned rubber getting back to her seat when she was through. I guess she's not exactly used to the limelight.

She's got plenty of company. Four more kids read their poetry for the first time today. They were shaking in their boots, but it was all good. I only had to tell one of them to loosen up. Guess you could call that progress!

Devon Hope

Jump Shot. What kind of name is that? Not mine, but try telling that to the brothers at school. That's all they ever call me.

You'd think it was written somewhere. Tall guys must be jocks. No. Make that tall *people,* 'cause Diondra's got the same problem. Everybody expects her to shoot hoops. The difference is, she's got no talent in that direction. Ask me, she's got no business playing b-ball. That's my game.

I've got good height and good hands, and that's a fact. But what about the rest of me? Forget who I really am, who I really want to be. The law is be cool, be tough, play ball, and use books for weight training—not reading. Otherwise, everybody gives you grief. Don't ask me why I care, especially when the grief is coming from a punk like Wesley. Judging from the company he keeps, he's a gangsta in sheep's clothing. I don't even know why he and Tyrone bother coming to school. It's clear they don't take it seriously, although maybe they're starting to. That's according to Sterling, who believes in praying for everybody and giving them the benefit of the doubt. I love the preacher-man, but I think he may be giving these brothers too much credit. Anyway, when I hang around after school and any of the guys ask me: "Yo, Devon, where you going?" I tell them I'm heading for the gym to meet Coach and work on my layup. Then once they're out the door, I cut upstairs to the library to sneak a read.

It's not much better at home. My older brother's always after me to hit the streets with him, calls me a girly man for loving books and jazz.

Don't get me wrong. B-ball is all right. Girls like you, for one thing. But it's not *you* they like. It's Mr. Basketball. And if that's not who you are inside, then it's not you they're liking. So what's the point? Still, I don't mind playing, just not all the time.

This year is looking better. My English teacher has got us studying the Harlem Renaissance, which means we have to read a lot of poetry. That suits me just fine, gives me a reason to drag around my beat-up volumes of Langston Hughes and Claude McKay. Whenever anybody bugs me about it, all I have to say is "Homework." Even so, I'd rather the brothers not catch me with my head in a book.

The other day, I duck into the library, snare a corner table, and hunker down with *3000 Years of Black Poetry*. Raynard sees me, but it's not like he's going to tell anybody. He hardly speaks, and he never hangs with any of the brothers I know. So I breathe easy. I'm sure no one else has spotted me until a head pops up from behind the stacks. It's Janelle Battle from my English class. I freeze and wait for the snickers I'm used to. Wait for her to say something like: "What? Coach got you *reading* now? Afraid you're gonna flunk out and drop off the team?" But all she does is smile and wave. Like it's no big deal for me to be in a library reading. Like I have a right to be there if I want. Then she pads over, slips a copy of *The Panther & the Lash* on my table, and walks away without saying a word. It's one of my favorite books by Langston Hughes. How could she know? Seems like she's noticed me in the library more often than I thought.

Janelle is all right. So what if she's a little plump? At least when you turn the light on upstairs, somebody's at home. She's smart, and she doesn't try hiding it. Which gets me thinking. Maybe it's time I quit sneaking in and out of the library like some thief. Maybe it's time I just started being who I am.

Bronx Masquerade

BY DEVON HOPE

I woke up this morning
exhausted from hiding
the me of me
so I stand here confiding
there's more to Devon
than jump shot and rim.
I'm more than tall
and lengthy of limb.
I dare you to peep
behind these eyes,
discover the poet
in tough-guy disguise.
Don't call me Jump Shot.
My name is Surprise.

Tyrone

Shoot. If I had moves like Devon, I'd be cruising crosscourt with Scotty Pippin! That's probably what the brotha's gonna end up doing, anyway, 'cause he ain't half the word-man I am. 'Course, I probably been at it longer.

He might get better. I said *might*. And who knows? Muhammad Ali was a boxer *and* a poet. Maybe it's time for another hoop-man to rise to the occasion and show Shaquille he ain't the only word-man on the court.

Lupe Algarin

Janelle's got a thing for Devon, but she ain't the only one. Last week I seen some girl named Beth in here staring at him like he was chocolate ice cream she couldn't wait to spoon up. She don't even belong in this class. Come to think of it, a lot of extra kids been showing up in our class on Open Mike Fridays. They heard about the poetry and they been coming to check it out. A bunch of teachers are getting mad at Mr. Ward with all these kids skipping their classes. Everybody's talking about it.

Poor Mr. Ward. He sends students back where they belong—when he catches them. Our class is big, though, and it's easy to duck down behind someone in the back of the room and hide. Sometimes we're halfway through the period before he notices someone who doesn't belong. But he caught Beth last week, and I saw Janelle grinning. She don't have Devon yet, but still she wants him all to herself. I know that feeling, when you love somebody like that. And not just a guy.

I love my Rosa.

Rosa is so beautiful. I wish I could bring her to school. Mr. Ward would love her. Her toes are like tiny *churros* you want to nibble all the time. And I do, whenever my big sister, Christina, has me over to baby-sit. She smiles more than she did before she had Rosa. Or maybe she's just happy to be out of the house. I would be. There's nothing for me there, that's for sure.

My brother, Tito, left long ago, and then Christina. So it's just me now, with Mami and her husband, Berto. Besides her factory job, all she cares about is him. As for Berto, he's got no use for nobody's kids, even Mami's.

Why does she put up with him? All he does is belch beer and scream at her to bring him and his buddies more while they sit around playing dominos or watching fights on TV.

"I bet Papi doesn't guzzle beer all the time," I often say to Mami.

"You don't know what he does, Lupe," she always says. "How could you? You were only five when he left. And he left on his own, Lupe. *Pero,* what did I expect? He was a *jíbaro* through and through. He couldn't *wait* to get back to his precious mountains! And this is the man you love? But Berto, who puts food in your mouth, him you despise. *¡Dios mio!*"

I hate it when she calls Papi a hick, the way she spits the word out.

I used to write him. So many letters. But he never wrote back. Why, Papi? There's nobody here to love me now. Mami has Berto, Tito has his *carnales* on the streets, Christina has Chooch and Rosa. And me? Raul's been giving me the eye lately, but he can forget it. He's too much in love with himself, always drawing pictures of his own face. What's that about? Besides, I already got a man. My Marco. Except, Marco hardly has time for me, even though he claims I'm his woman, his one and only.

Sometimes I say my rosaries and beg for someone to love. I lay in bed under the crucifix and pray 'til my fingers go numb on the beads.

Lately when I look at Rosa, I think I should do like my friend Gloria Martinez. I should make a baby of my own. Maybe that's the answer.

I like Marco good enough. I don't want to marry him, but he's cute. We'd make pretty babies together, I think.

I've always loved babies. When I was younger, I would wrap my doll in the lace from my first Communion and I'd show her off to all my neighbors. "*Mira, mira,*" I'd say. "See my baby. Isn't she perfect?" And she loved me better than anybody, because I was her mother. It was only pretend, of course. But if I had a real baby, she would love me like that. The way Gloria's baby loves her. The way Rosa loves Christina.

I saw Gloria and her baby in the grocery last night. I waved to them and all the time, I'm thinking, Gloria, you have no idea how lucky you are.

Brown Hands

BY LUPE ALGARIN

You, macho soledad,
the secret I whisper in the night,
you fill your eyes with me
like a mirror
I see myself in.
Our twin hearts beat
like congas, the rhythm
churning our blood
to salsa.
Our brown hands entwine
beneath moonshine,
clasping all the love
we'll ever need—

Tyrone

So, the daydreamer speaks.

Every time I look at Lupe, she seems like she's somewhere else. Or maybe she just wants to be. Maybe she's thinkin' about the guy in that poem. But if she is, how come she never smiles?

Gloria Martinez

Pampers. Apple sauce. Strained peas. I look up for a minute, see Lupe smiling at me. I nod, then go back to making my list. *Orange juice. Baby powder. Soy milk.* I didn't even know what soy milk *was* a year ago.

"Gloria." Raynard pokes me in the arm, gestures toward the front of the room. Mr. Ward is heading in my direction. I put my shopping list away before he can ask me what soy milk has to do with Zora Neale Hurston and the book he's been reading to us, *Their Eyes Were Watching God*. I turn to Raynard and nod thanks. He doesn't say much, but he always looks out for me.

I shoulda made a shopping list before I left the house this morning, but I barely got out as it is. Angel spit up on my shirt right when I was headed out the door. It's like he *picks* the time to do it. Like he doesn't want me to leave. It took me ten minutes to clean him up and find myself another shirt. If Mami hadn't done the laundry for me yesterday, I wouldn't even have a clean one to wear.

I was stupid to think I could do this on my own. Even with Mami's help, I hardly have time to study or do my homework. Last week, Lupe asked if I could hang out with her after school and I just about laughed in her face. *"Chica,"* I wanted to say, "them days are over for me." I go straight home now, except for maybe stopping at the grocery. It's no more *Gloria Loca,* party girl. Fun ain't even in my vocabulary anymore.

Once you have a kid, everything changes.

If I could go back, do things over . . . but I can't. No sense dreaming about it.

I love my Angel, and that's no lie. But I wish he didn't cry so much. He always wants something—his bottle, a new diaper, the teddy he dropped on the floor for the sixteenth time in a row. Or else he wants me to hold him, like I can rock a baby and write a paper at the same time! And forget about sleep. He wakes me up in the middle of the night so much, I practically wake up on my own now.

Two weeks ago, he wakes up crying with a fever. I don't know what to do. I rub him with cold washcloths, and then I take his temperature. I give him baby Tylenol, walk him up and down, and I take his temperature. I sing to him, I rock him, I give him a bottle of water, and take his temperature. I must've taken his temperature ten times before his fever finally broke. Then I put him in bed with me so I can watch him. By the time I close my eyes, the clock radio says 3:16 A.M. The next day, I have a math test. Which I flunk, of course. I keep nodding off between reading the problems and working out the solutions. I was a mess. Lucky for me, when I explained what happened, the teacher let me take the test over.

I still got two years to go before I graduate. But I've got to make it, and I've got to go to college. Period. Angel's father already told me straight-up he ain't having nothing to do with this baby, so it's on me. Mami says she'll help, but it's me who has to make a good life for Angel. It's like she says, my life ain't about just me anymore. It's about my son.

Lupe has no idea how lucky she is.

How can I get through to her?

Message to a Friend

BY GLORIA MARTINEZ

That girl in the mirror,
daughter of San Juan
made of sunshine and sugarcane,
looks like me.
She used to run, weightless,
Time a perfumed bottle
hanging from her neck,
mañana *a song*
she made up the words to
while she skipped—
until the day she stopped,
caught the toothless, squirming bundle
heaven dropped into her arms
and gravity kicked in.
Her life took a new spin.
This screaming gift did not
lead her to dream places
or fill all her empty spaces
like she thought.
Silly chica. *She bought into*
Hollywood's lie,

that love is mostly what you get
instead of what you give,
and what it costs,
like the perfumed bottle
ripped from her neck
and sent flying to the ground.
The crashing sound
of years lost
shattered in her ears,
and new fears emerged
from the looking glass.
Sometimes I wonder
if she'll ever sing again.

Tyrone

Girl's got a lot of heart, coming back to school after havin' a baby. I saw her around here last year. Man, did she get big! She shrunk right back down, though. She's fine, so I can see why a guy would want to give her a child. Not like any other guy will get the chance, the way she steers clear and keeps to herself.

Fine as she is, the girl ain't no dummy. Not writing poetry like that.

She should put it up on the wall. If you ask me, it belongs there.

Janelle Battle

"Janelle Hope. Mrs. Janelle Hope. Mrs. Devon Hope." Dream on, fool. You can stand here in the girls' room and practice saying that name 'til your tongue falls out, or the change bell rings, whichever comes first, and it still won't ever be true. Face it. Devon is Denzel Washington, and you are Thighs "R" Us.

I can hear Lupe now. "Stop putting yourself down. You have a very pretty face. Besides, you have a lot more going for you." Yeah, well, I guess that's true. I mean, I am smart and funny, and I know I'm a good person. But this is high school, and nobody seems to care about that. Why couldn't I be tall and elegant like Diondra, or have Judianne's perfect complexion, all smooth, super-rich fudge? Better yet, why couldn't I look like Tanisha, or Gloria? Then I might have a chance with somebody like Devon. But I don't, so forget it.

Devon is different from the other jocks, though.

How many guys you know read Claude McKay for fun? Seems like every time I go to the library, I catch him squeezed into a corner like he's got something to hide. He smiled at me last time I saw him there. That's something, isn't it? He didn't have to smile, even if I did smile and wave first. And he seemed to like the poem I read at the last Open Mike Friday.

I can't believe I'm getting up in front of people and talking about personal stuff, and liking it. I'm saying things that I would never tell anybody, usually. But, I don't know. There's something about reading poetry. It's almost like acting. The room is kind of set up like a stage, anyway. Mr. Ward turns most of the lights out, and we stand in a spot in front of the video camera. Once he switches it on, it's like you become somebody else, and you can say anything, as long as it's in a poem. Then, when you're finished, you just disappear into the dark and sit down, and you're back to being your own self. Gloria says it's the same for her.

"Hey, Janelle."

Oh, no. It's Miss Big Mouth Fifth Avenue in another one of her original getups. Where'd she come from?

"Hey, Judianne." I thought the bathroom was empty. How long was she there? I hope she didn't hear me talking to the mirror. That's all I need, to have the whole school laughing about me having a crush on Devon. Lord, please don't let that happen. It's bad enough they call me Battle of the Bulge behind my back.

I wish, I wish, I wish. God, I wish people could see me on the inside. I know I'm beautiful there.

inside

BY JANELLE BATTLE

Daily
I notice you frown
at my thick casing,
feel you poke me
with the sharp tip
of your booted words.
You laugh,
rap my woody shell
with wicked whispers shaped
like knuckles,
then toss me aside.
Lucky for me,
I don't bruise easily.
Besides,
your loss
is someone else's gain
for I am coconut,
and the heart of me
is sweeter
than you know.

Tyrone

You never think other folks got feelings. Like Janelle. I must've cracked wise a hundred times about her weight. Never even thought about it. It was just something I did for a laugh. Listening to her now, it don't seem all that funny.

Leslie Lucas

I'm starting to feel like I know Janelle, at least a little. And Lupe. And Gloria. And Raynard. Before Open Mike Fridays, I hardly knew anybody in this school at all. Big surprise.

What could I possibly have in common with these kids? I must've asked myself that question a million times a day when I moved here. I'm white, they're Black and Hispanic. I grew up in Westchester County. They grew up in New York City. I like Sheryl Crow, they like Lauryn Hill. Except for Raynard and Devon, who are into jazz. It's like we come from two different planets. But hey, it's not my fault. I didn't choose to be here. If it weren't for Mom up and dying on me, I'd still be back in Ossining with my friends.

I miss my friends. That's mostly why I hated moving here. I knew I wouldn't have anybody to talk to when it hurts, and it hurts all the time. Missing Mom, I mean. I was full up with loneliness for her a few weeks ago. It was one of those moments that come from outta nowhere, when you all of a sudden feel something reach inside your chest, grab your heart, and squeeze 'til you can hardly breathe. I was in the girls' locker room at the time, and for a minute, I wheeled around like Uncle Donny does when he's drunk. That's when I bumped into Porscha Johnson.

Porscha Johnson has the reputation for being a little touched in the head. In freshman year, she'd beaten the snot out of a girl who'd pushed her too far. They say it took four people to pull her off of the other girl. Everybody had pretty much steered clear of her since then. This is who I bump into.

"Hey! Watch it," she said.

"Sorry," I told her.

"You got that right. Why don't you sorry yourself on outta here?" Usually, this would be the cue for me to make myself invisible, but I was hurting too bad, and I was not in the mood. I flung my locker door open and spoke between my teeth.

"I said I was sorry. Now why don't you just leave me alone?"

"Leave you alone? Look, if you wanted to be left alone, why the hell did you invade *my* space?"

By space, I thought she meant neighborhood. That's when I felt my head spin off. "My mom died, all right? And I was sent to live with my grandmother, who lives in this neighborhood, and I had no choice. Not that it's any of your business."

The split second those last words flew out, I wanted to take them back, but I couldn't. I swallowed hard and waited for Porscha to shove me against the lockers, or to punch me in the stomach, or to whip out a knife like I'd seen kids do on TV. Instead, she stepped back, lowered herself to the bench, and said, "Sorry about your mom. My mom died too."

Turns out we both live with our grandmothers. For a long time, she put off telling me what her mom died from. My mom died of cancer, which was no big secret, but hers died from a drug overdose. Porscha thought that would make a difference, but when I found out, I told her it made no difference at all. Dead is dead, and lonely is lonely, and they both stink. All that matters, I told her, is that we're friends. And we are.

I'm lucky. I was on my way to being like Amy Moscowitz, the one girl in class almost nobody knows anything about. She cuts herself off, hardly ever speaks, or lets anyone in. She seems to be happy by herself, but I need to hear somebody's voice besides my own. I'm not as strong as she is, and now I don't have to pretend that I am.

Open Mike Fridays help. We kind of have our own little clique now. The whole school knows who we are, that we're "the poets." It's weird. For the first time in my life, I'm part of a group that's cool. Who would believe it?

Last month, Mr. Ward gave our class an assignment to write a poem about what frightens us most, in honor of Halloween. A year ago, I might have written about something silly, like ghosts, which I don't even believe in, and even if I did, ghosts would not be at the top of my list. The scariest thing I can think of now is being all alone in the world.

Common Ground

BY LESLIE LUCAS

On the dark side of the moon
where death comes sooner
than expected;
at the edge of heartbreak
we both take
a leap
into the unknown;
at the center of loneliness
we dip into a pool
of tears
and thrash around
desperate not to drown;
we both reach out
for a life preserver,
something to hold on to
something sturdy
something new.
That's when we see it,
a buoy called friendship
bobbing up between us

and we swim toward it
for all we are worth
and we meet there,
somewhere
    in the middle.

Tyrone

Man, that little white girl be getting pretty deep. I figured her for something lame like "Roses are red, violets are blue." Glad I didn't have a bet on that action.

More than half the class wanted to read today, but most of them were girls. I wish a few more of the brothas would step up to the mike, even this thing out a little. Know what I'm saying?

Judianne Alexander

Good thing Leslie's cough woke me in class this morning. I nodded off three times. Once more and Mr. Ward said he'd be bringing me a pillow. That's what I get for staying up late. Again.

What choice did I have? Open Mike Friday is today and I am not about to stand in front of the class in some funky old outfit. I didn't realize it would take me half the night to finish something new. I hope I can stay awake long enough to read my poem when my turn comes.

Me, writing poetry! What a scream. I'm not smart enough to be writing poetry in the first place, though Mr. Ward says I'm smarter than I know. Yeah, well, I wouldn't have bothered trying to write anything except that Open Mike Friday is one time I know I can get Tyrone Bitting's attention, and I've got a thing for Tyrone. Of course, he's got a thing for Tanisha Scott—like every other boy in school.

Too bad we can't all have good hair and light skin. Who am I kidding? She's more than that. She's pretty. Which I'm not, as my stepfather reminds me ten times a day. Like I don't know that from looking in the mirror, or from having kids tease me about my blue-black skin all the way through school. But my body's good. Nothing wrong with me in that department. That's why I got to show it off, wear clothes that accentuate the positive. The shorter, the better. And I don't even have to buy them. I can make them myself. It ain't much, but that's one thing I learned from my mother. How to sew.

Last week, I wore my patchwork denim skirt and vest with the red leather pockets that just about broke my sewing machine needle. Sheila was all up in my face, telling me how cool I looked, like I needed her opinion. Why she's always trying to kiss up to Black people is beyond me. Anyway, it was Lupe's compliment I listened to. She took one look at my outfit and told me she was jealous. Said she wished she could sew like me. Honey, I thought to myself, give me some of that pretty skin and hair of yours, and I'll trade.

Lupe has no idea how pretty she is. You should see Raul and some of the other guys—Black *and* white—sniffing round her. And does she notice? Don't look like it to me. Except for Raul. It's hard not to notice Mr. Latin Loverboy. Anyway, Lupe says she already has a boyfriend. I'm thinking he's invisible, though. I never see him. He goes to another school, she says. Others say he doesn't go to school at all, that he dropped out a long time ago, that he's eight years older than Lupe. Eight years! But hey, it's none of my business. At least she's got somebody. I'm still working on that one. Meanwhile, I spend my weekends alone, holed up in a room with my Singer sewing machine.

I've been helping Mom mark and cut out patterns for as long as I can remember. I even helped her draw a few that Vogue never thought of. They should take a look at my sketch pad! Now, if I could just figure out how to design poetry as well as I design clothing, I could turn myself into somebody special. Wouldn't that be a neat trick?

It wouldn't hurt if I could come up with something deep to write about, like Chankara. I wouldn't want to have the experience of someone beating up on me, though. It's bad enough my stepfather talks about me like a dog. The few times my mother gets on him about it, he laughs it off and says he's just joking. I should cut his tongue out, see how funny he thinks that is, 'cause there's sure nothing funny about being called ugly. So why does Mom let him do it? Sometimes I think she loves him more than me. Otherwise, she wouldn't let him tear me down like that.

One of these days, he's going to call me ugly, and I'm going to ugly myself on outta there. I don't know where I'll go, but it'll be far away from him. Then Mom won't have to worry about defending me. And I won't have to waste energy being angry because she hardly ever does.

She's all right in private, though. She tells me to ignore my stepfather, says I've got a lot to work with, that I can make myself over with hair and makeup. When I'm older. For now, I can barely get out of the house with lipstick. Meanwhile, I sit at my sewing machine and dream about the great transformation I'm going to make someday. As if I could use pinking shears to cut out a new face for myself.

Right. Dream on.

Cocoon

BY JUDIANNE ALEXANDER

Her cocoon is see-through.
Inside, she is busy
with pattern and pinking shears.
If the ears are too long,
she'll snip them.
If the mouth is too wide,
she'll stitch up the corners.
Her needle and thread
hold more magic
than any wand.
With her chalk,
she can outline
a fine and voluptuous shape.
The nape of the neck
is a perfect place
to tuck and fold.
Her straight pins hold
the skin together, just so.
A quick basting stitch
lets her know where
to set her seams,

her cuffs, her hem.
After all, her arms and legs
mustn't be too long.
She mustn't stand too tall.
Perfect beauty is what
she's after.
She's already had enough
laughter in her life.
The day she clips her way
out of her cocoon,
the only sound
she plans to hear
is a deafening cheer.

Tyrone

Don't none of these girls like the way they look? I
don't get it. Guys don't have that problem. Not the
guys I know. Would somebody clue me in?

Lupe

Judianne tapped me on the shoulder this morning and passed me a note real quick before Mr. Ward could see. It was from Leslie. "Are you okay?" it said. I turned and flashed her my "okay" smile. The smile was for real. I'm fine today. *Pero*, last night? Forget it. I broke up with Marco and I was a mess.

It was so silly. I been planning to break up with him for weeks. I mean, I hardly ever seen him anyways. Plus, I've been thinking, if I'm ever going to have a baby, I need to find a better father than Marco, somebody who's got time for me, at least. I don't want my baby and me to be alone, like Gloria and Angel. She got it harder than I thought. Still, I wasn't in no hurry to break up with Marco, because that would make it official: Lupe Algarin is alone. I can't hardly breathe thinking about it.

I busted up with Marco over the phone, which is good because, right after I hung up, I felt this big hole rip open inside of me, and I started crying like little Rosa does when she's hungry and her bottle is empty and her mom has just left the room. Once I calmed down, I called Leslie. But as soon as I heard her voice, the tears started coming again.

"I'm sorry," I said, trying to hide my sniffles. "I shouldn't have called."

"Lupe, what's wrong?"

"I don't want to bother you."

"You're not bothering me. Anyway, that's what friends are for. Now, what happened?"

I told her about Marco, and how I left him, and how he didn't even seem to care that much, and how I was all alone now. She was quiet for a minute. Then she said, "Lupe, sounds to me like you were already alone."

"I know, but—"

"Never mind. It's okay. You're not really alone, anyhow. You have friends. You have me."

"Yeah. I guess."

Leslie said she feels lonely sometimes too. She told me about how it was right after her mom died. I really listened because she doesn't talk about her mother much. She said that after the funeral, and even months after she moved in with her grandmother, her world felt so empty and hollow, she could hold it at one end and ring it like a bell. It's better now, she said.

We must've talked for an hour. I can't remember half of what we talked about, except that Leslie said friends can be like *familia*. Only she pronounced it *fama-lea*. It took me a minute to figure out what she meant. Anyway, she was right.

So I don't have a boyfriend now. So what? Neither does Janelle. Or Gloria. Or Leslie. But we have each other.

Maybe we can all be alone together.

El Noche

BY LUPE ALGARIN

I stand out in the cold
el noche *and I*
both too lonely for whispers.
Only the wind
shatters this silence.
I have been here before
choking in solitude,
but this time
when all the earth
is hollow as a bell,
I hold one end,
ring it,
and you come—
a pale-skinned surprise,
a friend.

Tyrone

Her voice is so soft, I close my eyes every time she reads, trying to hold in the sound a little longer. I'm glad Mr. Ward asked her to read her piece over again. She says it like a whisper, but it's powerful stuff. That's one thing these ladies know how to do. Be soft and strong at the same time. Like my moms.

Janelle

Tyrone said something to me today, but I didn't hear him. I'm having trouble getting Judianne's poem out of my head. Even Lupe said it was a surprise. We all thought Miss Fifth Avenue was self-confidence with a capital S, but her poem was all about wishing she could make herself over. I know what that's like. Which is what I tried telling Judianne the other day. Boy, was *that* a mistake!

I ran into her in the bathroom. That seems to be our place to meet. Anyway, I decided to take advantage of the meeting.

"I've been meaning to tell you, I really liked the poem you read for Open Mike Friday."

"Yeah? Well, thanks. I'm not used to writing poetry."

"Well, nobody could tell it. You know, I could really get into what you were saying about trying to make yourself over, wishing you could be perfect and all. I mean, I feel like that every time I look in the mirror."

Judianne nodded, and her tight mouth softened a little. She was about to say something, but then a toilet flushed and she realized we were not alone. Sheila Gamberoni came out of the stall, and the minute she did, Judianne slipped back behind her usual scowl and turned mean.

"Look, I am nothing like you, okay?" she spit out. "In case you haven't noticed, you're fat and I'm not. And you're wrong about my poem. It was just words. It didn't mean anything. You got that?" And she slammed out of the bathroom and left me there, stinging from the inside out.

I bit my lip to keep the tears back. I turned the faucet on and washed my hands a few times, staring at the sink until I heard Sheila step out into the hall. I glanced up at the mirror before I left. "You're wrong, Judianne," I said to the mirror. "They weren't just words, and you know it."

I haven't tried talking with her since. I don't want to give her an excuse to be mean to me again. I'm not mad at her, though. I know there's a part of her that's as scared to look in the mirror as I am. I saw that person for a few seconds, even if she wants to deny it. Calling me names won't change the way she feels inside. One of these days, she's going to find that out.

Mirror, Mirror

BY JANELLE BATTLE

Sisters under the skin,
we meet in the mirror,
our images superimposed
for one split second.
Ready or not,
I peer into your soul
and dive deep,
splash-landing
in a pool of pain
as salty and familiar
as the tears on my cheek.
Your eyes don't like
what I see.
You don't want to be me.
So you curse
and smash the mirror,
which gets you what?
A bit of blood,
a handful of glass splinters,
another source of pain.

Tyrone

Mm, mm, mm. Janelle is working it. Seems like her pieces are getting tighter. Actually, I think everybody's getting better. Practice makes perfect, I guess, and we be getting plenty of practice these days. Mr. Ward had to switch Open Mike from once a month to once a week 'cause so many people be wanting to read their work.

I b'lieve there's more to this thing than Mr. Ward planned on. But he's cool. He keeps rolling with it.

Tanisha Scott

If Tyrone calls me "caramel cutie" one more time, I'll scream. I turn to cut my eyes at him and find Judianne staring at me again. Even after I turn away, I can feel her eyes stroking the back of my head. I'm so sick of people making a big deal over my "good hair."

I caught her pawing my hair just last week. I reached back and grabbed a finger before she had a chance to pull away. I spun around, more aggravated than angry, and said, "Look, it's just hair. It's not magic, so don't go rubbing it for good luck. Trust me, it hasn't brought me any." Raynard stifled a laugh. You never know when that boy is paying attention. Of course, Judianne made out like she didn't know what I was talking about, swearing up and down she hadn't touched a single hair on my head. But I'd seen that hungry look in her eyes, like I had something she wanted. It was the same look my cousin Faith always gives me just before she says "I sure wish I had good hair like yours" or "I wish I was light like you," followed by "then boys would like me better." Which isn't true, if you ask me. But try telling that to my cousin. Or to Judianne. If she doesn't quit bugging me, I'm gonna ask Mr. Ward to change my seat.

She's why I chopped all my hair off last year. Well, people like her.

My mother freaked when she saw me. My bangs were cut straight across my brow and the sides were sort of squared at the neck. I looked like a clown minus the red nose. It was the best I could do on my own. And it looked better than that time I washed it in detergent to kink it up so I could have an Afro like my cousins. Anyway, Mom hated it so much, she finally forked over money for a visit to a hair salon to have it cut professionally.

Served her right. I'd begged her to let me cut it off before. "But your hair is so beautiful," she'd say. "Why would you want to cut it?"

My mind flashed to the school cafeteria that afternoon. I'd walked past a group of would-be girlfriends who sucked their teeth at me and said my name like it was curdled milk they couldn't wait to spit out. "Here come Miss High-Yella, thinkin' she's all that, with her so-called 'good hair,'" said one. "Far's I'm concerned, she ain't nothin'," said another. "Less than nothin'," said a third. I shook off the memory.

"Look, Mom," I said. "You don't understand." But she wasn't listening.

"Most girls you know would kill to have your hair," she said.

"That's just it, Mom. They hate me for it and they hate my skin. I can't do anything about my skin, okay, but my hair I can fix." I lost the argument, of course. Then, three weeks later, I cut it anyway.

It's growing back now and I've decided to let it. I mean, it's not like I can win, you know? I've tried dressing down in T-shirts and baggy pants, with no makeup, and it's still either "Come here, pretty mama" from cocky boys like Wesley who I have absolutely no use for, or getting grief from girls I used to want as friends. I even thought about getting brown contact lenses once, to cover up my green eyes, but my friend Sterling talked me out of it. He's light-skinned too, so he knows where I'm coming from. He said he used to twist himself into a pretzel over it until he realized God loves him just the way he is. Besides, he told me, if I did start wearing colored contacts, those girls would only say I was trying to be something I'm not, and he's right. So I give up. Let 'em say what they want. I am not a skin color or a hank of wavy hair. I am a person, and if they don't get that, it's their problem, not mine.

I'm better off with friends like Diondra and Janelle who know I'm more than what I look like. They know I've got a brain, and I know how to use it. They're no dummies either. That's why I asked Mr. Ward if the three of us could do a group project on

Women of the Harlem Renaissance for extra credit. We had our first meeting at my house.

"Can we do Zora Neale Hurston?" asked Janelle. "I know we read *Their Eyes Were Watching God* in class, but she wrote a bunch of other stuff too."

"You're right," I said. "Good idea." I picked up my pad and wrote Z. Hurston at the top. "Okay. That's a good start, but I think we should cover some women you don't hear so much about."

"Like?"

"Georgia Douglas Johnson. I read some of her work in a book called *3000 Years of Black Poetry*. I'd never heard of her before, and I bet nobody else in class has either."

"Cool," said Diondra. "Maybe I should read that book and see if I can get a couple of ideas."

"You can borrow it from the library," I said. "Soon as I return it, that is." We all laughed. I'm notorious for turning library books in late. "Meanwhile, Diondra, you can start working on portraits of these sisters so we can use them for our report covers when we're done."

I didn't wait for her to volunteer, because I knew she wouldn't. For somebody who has talent, she spends an awful lot of energy hiding it. But I figure if enough people tell her she's good, she'll start believing it. That means people actually have to *see* her work. I'm going to make sure they do, even if I have to keep volunteering her for projects 'til we graduate.

She's not about to say no to me. She knows I'm stubborn when I want something.

"Fine," says Diondra. "I'll do the portraits, but don't look at me when Mr. Ward sees those report covers and busts out laughing."

"Laughing? What do you mean, laughing?" Janelle and I looked at each other. I nodded, and on the count of three, we jumped on Diondra and tickled her 'til tears of laughter squirted out of her eyes.

Them's my girls. They don't care what I look like. They know the only difference between my color and theirs is that the slave master who owned my family raped my great-great-grandma instead of theirs. And like my dad says, that ain't nothing to celebrate or be stuck up about.

For the Record

BY TANISHA SCOTT

It's the blood that tells:
slaves black as Mississippi mud
ring the trunk
of my family tree.
They speak through me
Black as they want to be.
The slaver's white drop
couldn't stop the spread
of African cells.
They're bred
in the bone,
past the slick hair,
the too-fair skin.
So don't tell me
I can't fit in.
My heart beats
like a talking drum,
my mom hums to Bessie
just like yours,
the brothers in my dreams

are pure ebony,
and blue-black grandmother arms
like the ones
that cradled my ancestors
have often cradled me.

Tyrone

Now I know why the sista hisses every time I call her "caramel cutie." That'd be the last thing she wants to hear! She's proud of her African self, and I'm down with that. That's why I be wearing my *kufi* every chance I get.

I wonder if the sista's into African music. I gotta ask her about that sometime. Maybe I could hook up some African drum music to go with her poetry for the assembly Teach told us about. She could read her stuff, and I could play DJ. Yeah! I could get into that.

Devon

I look up from my lunch tray and catch Tanisha's eye while she stands in the cafeteria line. We nod.

"Yo, brotha," says Tyrone, thinking I'm nodding to him. I wave and turn away.

Tanisha is one fine sister, but I never say that to her face. She gets tired of hearing it from all the other guys. They look at her and that's all they see, what's on the surface. That's what she told me when we talked once after Open Mike Friday. We talked about superficial judgments, how people look at you and think they know who you are, what you are, how they put you in a box: jock, china doll, whatever. That's one thing me and Tanisha got in common. We know all about being put in a box. I feel like I'm gonna be climbing out of the one marked "dumb jock" all my life.

"Hey, Jump Shot," I hear somebody call me from behind. It's Mike from the basketball team. I nod, then go back to reading Imamu Amiri Baraka's *Preface to a Twenty Volume Suicide Note*. Mike slams his tray down beside me and sits.

"What's that you reading?"

"Baraka," I tell him. "Poetry."

"Oh. Right. You got that class."

At first I don't say anything. Then I decide. "No, man. It's not for class. I'm reading it for me, actually."

"You gots to be kiddin'."

"No."

"That's so lame, man."

I keep my finger in the book and turn to face him.

"You ever read Baraka?" No answer. "You should check him out."

"Hey, do what you want, man. I ain't interested." Mike picks up his tray and moves to another table, shaking his head. I go back to my reading, seeing as how he'd given me *permission* and all.

Forget this. Tonight our team plays Bronx Science. When I get on the bus with the rest of the guys, I'm taking a copy of Baraka's book with me to read, and I'm gonna make sure everybody sees it. Especially Mike.

Black Box

BY DEVON HOPE

In case I forgot to tell you,
I'm allergic to boxes:
Black boxes, shoe boxes
New boxes, You boxes—
Even cereal boxes
Boasting champions.
(It's all a lie.
I've peeked inside
And what I found
Were flakes.)
Make no mistake,
I make no exceptions
For Cracker Jack
Or Christmas glitter.
Haven't you noticed?
I'm made of skeleton,
Muscle and skin.
My body is the only box
I belong in.
But you like your boxes
So keep them.

Mark them geek, wimp, bully.
Mark them china doll, brainiac,
Or plain dumb jock.
Choose whatever
Box you like, Mike.
Just don't put me
In one, son.
Believe me,
I won't fit.

Tyrone

The brotha's right. I look around this class and nobody I see fits into the box I used to put them in. Startin' with Mr. Ward. I figured him for a lightweight do-gooder who would last about five minutes in this neighborhood. But he stuck, and he got this poetry thing going. He even reads his own stuff sometimes. He's okay.

Devon's okay too. I don't know how bright the other jocks are, but there's nothing dumb about this brotha. Mr. Ward says you have to take people one at a time, check out what's in their head and heart before you judge.

Word.

Sterling S. Hughes

Devon shook his head when he saw me standing in the lunch line yesterday, fingering an imaginary fret, making the appropriate sound effects. Friend or not, he thinks I'm crazy, but the brother behind me got into it, snapping his fingers to the rhythm I set. "Yeah!" he said. "Preacher got it goin' on."

My name is Sterling Samson, but everyone calls me Preacher. I intend to become a science teacher, not a preacher, but I don't mind being called one. Just so long as you don't call me Samson. I'm hoping to end up in a little better shape than he did.

I turned to the brother behind me and eased into a smile. "I play a real guitar at church every Sunday. You ought to come by and check me out sometime." Judging by the way the brother cut his eyes at me, his appearance on the steps of First Baptist Church seemed highly unlikely. Still, you never know.

I went back to my invisible string playing to keep my fingers limber for later. I had promised to hold the bass line for some of the brothers reading at this week's Open Mike. Mr. Ward was kind enough to lock my guitar up in his office in the morning so I wouldn't have to worry about it walking away before then.

Assuming I made it to his class without any trouble.

A brother named Leon "accidentally" bumped into me as I approached the cashier. He spilled, or should I say poured, a cupful of honey on my shoes. My *new* shoes.

"Oops! Looks like Mr. Goody Two-shoes got a mess to clean up," he said, laughing. His buddies joined in.

I stared down at my shoes, counting. *One. Two. Three. Four.* By the time I reached ten, I realized counting was not going to suffice.

I need you, Lord. Hold back the Samson in me. I may not have his strength, but you know I have his temper.

I counted backward from ten, felt my breath slowly evening out. A still, small voice reminded me to return good for evil, reminded me that my plans for the future do not include fisticuffs or expulsion. I am college-bound and nothing is going to keep me from it. Besides, these poor fools are only trying to get a rise out of me. They're only trying to prove that the peace of God is nonexistent. But how can they?

I looked up at Leon and shook my head. Then I grabbed him by the shoulders, kissed him loudly on both cheeks, and gave him a bear hug.

"Get off me, man!" he said, trying to pull away.

When I finally let him go, I whispered, "Leon, I forgive you." Fear blotted out the pupils in his eyes.

"Man," he yelled, "you some kind of freak!"

I smiled, strummed my imaginary guitar, and sang, "I'll be a fool for Christ, not just once, but twice." Leon and his friends backed away as if I'd set a match to them. They put as much distance between us as possible.

"You sick, man," Leon called over his shoulder. "Stay away from me!"

It's always something with these guys. Either they're trying to draw me into an infantile game of The Dozens so we can trade insults left and right, or they're slapping porno pictures inside my locker hoping to set me off. If they had some direction in their lives like Raul, Devon, or Raynard, they wouldn't have time to worry about me one way or the other. Which is precisely why I want to teach, to give young brothers like Leon some direction. Even Wesley has direction, although the brother could clean up his language. Sometimes he sounds like a thug in training. Leon's not much better.

If only Leon and his friends knew how lame their antics are. As if any of that could stop me from believing in God.

All my life, I've seen my mother pray, and all my life, I've seen her prayers answered. There was the time my baby brother was dying of pneumonia and the doctors had given up, but she prayed until the fever broke. There was the time she was laid off from her job, and the refrigerator was empty, and she bowed her head over an empty pot and prayed for God to fill it. That night, a woman upstairs begged her to accept a bag of frozen meats and vegetables, because she was moving the next day, and she hated to see good food go to waste. We had steaks that night, and we *never* have steaks. There were lots of times like that. "See there," Mom would say. "That's God's hand. If you have God's hand on your life, everything will be all right." So of course I believe. And I believe big. I'm believing God's going to get me and my three brothers into manhood, into college, and off of these streets—with no more than maybe a couple of black eyes between us. How's that for believing?

The change bell rang and I was still cleaning off my shoes. I could've used a few extra minutes to work on my own poem. It took me a while to get into this whole poetry thing, not that I don't like it. I read *God's Trombones* by James Weldon Johnson, and some of the work by Countee Cullen, like "Simon the Cyrenian Speaks," and I liked what the brothers had to say, but their styles don't suit me. Then Mr. Ward turned me onto Rev. Pedro Pietri, who is more my speed, even if he is kind of old. He knows how to put God and the street in the same sentence, and I figured if I'm going to write poetry at all, that's what I want to do. So I put together a few. I couldn't tell if they were any good, but I decided to read one anyway. If I get a laugh, it won't be the first time.

The bell rang one last time. I took a few bites of my sandwich, wrapped up the rest, and tossed it in my book case for later. I told my growling stomach to be quiet and headed to Mr. Ward's office for my guitar.

D-Train

BY STERLING S. HUGHES

He squeezed through the subway doors
a young gun, thirsty for the kind of coke
you can't sip through a straw.
He sized up the passengers,
chose his prey:
a wrinkled woman at the tail end
of her Geritol years
who fears her own shadow
with good reason.
He lunged at her,
demanded her cash
to replenish his stash
of powdered death.
No one blinked or came
to her aid, at first.
Then, in He beamed.
Light streamed from His fingers,
singed anyone caught without
a robe of righteousness
across his back.
The lack of goodness

in the young gun's heart
was oxygen to the fire, and so
he burned a good long while
before I woke.
The dream stoked my faith
in the judgment and justice
that will come someday
or this afternoon.
Soon. I turn up the collar
of my white robe,
relieved to know
God's got me covered
'cause I'm good,
but not that good.

Tyrone

The brotha took me to a whole other place. I'm not sure I got all of it, but I got that he don't call himself no angel. 'Course, if Mr. Goody Two-shoes ain't no angel, what does that make me? Never mind.

He sure worked that rhythm. I know that much. He snuck a little rhyme in there too. I like that. Go on, Preacher! Look like God got hisself a poet!

Diondra

I spent way too long yakking with Tanisha over lunch. She couldn't stop talking about Pedro Pietri, the poet Mr. Ward had invited to visit our class. He was coming in a couple of weeks and Tanisha said he was gonna rock the house. He was the only poet Mr. Ward had us read who we were actually going to meet, which was pretty cool. Tanisha could hardly wait to check him out. I had other things on my mind, though, so I was glad Tyrone came over and broke up the conversation. He started hitting on Tanisha, as usual. I whispered, "Sorry," and took off.

Ten more minutes and Mr. Ward will be in here. I flip my sketchbook open to a fresh page, clip my father's photo to the corner, and get busy. A few strokes of my pencil and the oval of his face is done. Then I start with his chin, I don't know why. Maybe because the hardness is there and I want to get it out of the way, hurry on to the softer parts of his face. The parts that show love. I've never done a portrait from the bottom to the top before, but why not? As long as it looks like my father when I'm done.

The first bell rings. I lift my head and there's Sterling, staring over my shoulder.

"Hey."

"Hey." I lean back so he can get a better look. "I just started this one," I tell him. Other kids file in, so I gather up my charcoal pencils.

Raul swirls his brushes in a jar of water and finishes straightening up Mr. Ward's desk. I catch his eye and we smile at each other. He's part of the reason I don't mind people looking at my drawings anymore. I guess I should give Tanisha some credit too. It was her bright idea to have me do those book report covers.

The day we got our reports back, Mr. Ward held mine up so everyone could see the cover. I tried evaporating on the spot, I swear. The last thing I wanted was extra attention. Too late! When class was over, I ran out of the room before anyone had a chance to laugh in my face, but Raul caught me in the hall and snatched the report from me quicker than a subway door slamming shut. He said he wanted to get a better look at it. I bit my tongue and stared at the floor.

"This is good!" he said. "Especially the eyes. They look right through you. You gotta show me how you do the eyes."

My jaw dropped. "You think they're that good?"

"You're kidding, right?" Raul didn't wait for an answer. He handed me back the report, shaking his head. "Wish I could do eyes like that. Anyway, see you later."

I looked down at my book cover as if I was seeing it for the first time. Raul was right. The drawing *was* good. The eyes *did* look right through you. Maybe I should try working on the rest of the face, I thought. I could do studies of mouths and noses and chins. I could try different kinds of faces, different shapes. I could get Mom to model for me. Or Tanisha. Or I could use pictures. We only have a bazillion photo albums around my house. Maybe I could bring one of them to school with me. Or I could just borrow a few of the pictures and then put them back later. Maybe . . .

I had a hard time concentrating on my classes that afternoon.

The next day, I wolfed down my lunch and half ran to Mr. Ward's room with a sketch pad and charcoal pencils. By the time Raul arrived, I was already at work. Nowadays I'm in here two, three times a week. I'd come more often, but I gotta make time for my friends.

I shade in my father's jawline just as Mr. Ward enters the room, then put my pencil down and look up in case he tries to catch my eye.

"Mr. Ramirez," says Mr. Ward, "may I have my desk, please?" Raul bows deep, like some actor in an old-time movie, then struts to his seat. He passes me on the way, leans down, eyes my rough sketch, and whispers, "Let me know when you get to the eyes."

My smile is so wide, my cheeks hurt.

High Dive

BY DIONDRA JORDAN

A trip to the city pool
ain't what it used to be.
I left the kiddy pool behind
many moons ago.
I know how to float
how to dog paddle
how to hold my breath
between breaststrokes.
I know the stench and sting
of chlorine.
It's no big thing.
But this,
scaling the ladder
for the high dive
drives me to distraction.
What if
I forget to swim?
What if
there's no water in the pool?
But wait.
Is it really water

I'm after?
I reach the top,
pad to the edge of the board,
and peek.
There it is,
swirls of blue, purple,
and periwinkle watercolor.
The perfect palette.
I take a deep breath,
dip the tip of my brush
into sky,
take one long leap
and . . .
To be continued.

Tyrone

I've been thinking we should plan on having a poetry slam next year. I ran the idea past Diondra. She's one of the shyest sistas in our class. At least, she was when school got started. Anyway, I figure if she's into the idea, everybody else should be down with it.

Next thing I need to do is pitch it to Mr. Ward, see if he can get the principal to go for it. Man, I would love to get in some guys from Bronx Science, or one of them other special schools, and turn them into toast at a poetry slam. There's no *way* they'd beat us. They wouldn't even know what hit 'em!

Amy Moscowitz

Amy. The name is petite, like me. It's also soft. I'm not. Just ask Tyrone. Or Diondra. Or Sterling. Better yet, ask my father. He thinks I'm so tough, I don't need anybody. Not even him. He didn't always treat me that way. He used to handle me more like china. But then Mom left to start another family—without us. After the divorce, Dad decided we both needed to toughen up, that we needed to learn to stand on our own. I thought he meant together.

Two years ago I got sick at school and he was called in to take me to the hospital. Apparently I had appendicitis. I was doubled over with pain, tears streaming down my face, and he wouldn't even put his arm around me. He just walked beside me, stiff as a two-by-four, asking "Are you okay?" every couple of minutes. Jerk.

Would it have killed him to touch me? To help me up the hospital stairs? Never mind. I won't bother needing anyone like that again.

Too bad my father's not more like Mr. Ward. His

daughter goes to this school, and I saw the two of them in the cafeteria the other day. I hear they have lunch together three times a week. Anyhow, there they were in the lunch line, him with his arm draped over her shoulder, the two of them blabbing away like old buddies. She was bent over a little, from the weight of her backpack I guess, and when he noticed, he slipped it off and carried it for her. She smiled up at him and gave his waist a squeeze, and I felt my stomach turn.

For about a minute, I hated that girl.

Sterling says jealousy is a waste of energy, that I should focus on what I have, not what I don't. That's what I get for opening my big mouth and telling him how I feel. But he's so easy to talk to, sometimes I let things slip before I even realize my mouth is open. Anyway, he's too busy trying to save my Jewish soul to think about betraying my secrets. He knows I'd never forgive him, and then where would he be? He could pretty much forget about preaching love and forgiveness around me after that. Not that all his preaching will get him anywhere, seeing as I'm an atheist. Still, his trying doesn't bother me, he's so up front about it.

He's right about the jealousy, though. I seem to be jealous of everyone and everything. Especially the friendships I see all around me. Leslie and Porscha, Lupe and Gloria, Tanisha and Diondra. It's enough to make me ill.

It's been forever since I had a best friend, let alone a boyfriend.

"Friendships don't just happen," Sterling tells me whenever I complain. "You have to reach out and make them."

"How?" I ask him.

"Just be yourself."

Myself. That's a laugh. If I were to show anyone who I really am inside, how cold my heart is, they'd probably run in the opposite direction. I tell Sterling this and he says, "Maybe. Maybe not. You won't know unless you try."

Sterling's right. I haven't been trying. Not since my parents divorced. I've been afraid to get close to anyone. When my mom left, I was suddenly out of orbit. It's like she was the sun, and when she took off, the only thing left was a big black hole where she used to be. Now the idea of letting somebody else get that close . . . I don't know. I'm just not ready. I wonder if I ever will be.

Ode to Stone

BY AMY MOSCOWITZ

One day at Far Rockaway
is all it took.
One look at rocks in water
decided me:
I want to be stone.
I want to be marble.
Dressed up limestone
never looked so good.
Let me be granite
and I promise
I'll show you how to take
a shellacking.
Yes, I'll risk sunburn.
Just let me be rock
wedged into the earth or sea
tidal waves crashing over me
while I remain intact—
no split at the core,
more buffed than bruised.
Forget the pillar of salt.

I'll look back at the count of three
and you can turn me into stone.
Go on.
I'm half rock
already.

Tyrone

Man! That girl is as cold as the snow on the ground. Somebody must've put a hurting on her. "I want to be stone." Can you get next to that? I've felt that way a couple of times. Once, when the undertaker carried my pops out of here. Another time when my girlfriend left me for my supposed-to-be homey. Both times I remember wishing I couldn't feel the hurt, wishing I could just cut my heart out and be done with it. But I like the way Amy said it. Let me be stone.

Sheila Gamberoni

Amy Moscowitz looked at me like I had two heads. Why? Just because I wanted to change my name.

When Mr. Ward took attendance this morning and got to me, I raised my hand and interrupted.

"Please don't call me Sheila," I said. "I prefer Natalina, my Africana name."

"Excuse me?" said Mr. Ward.

I cleared my throat, and spoke a little louder. "Please call me Natalina from now on."

Mr. Ward looked puzzled. "I'm sorry. I don't understand. Why would you—never mind, Sheila. Just see me after class."

I nodded. Diondra Jordan caught my eye and shook her head. Then she turned back to the charcoal portrait I saw her working on when I got to class. She slipped it into her notebook and shook her head again. I looked away just in time to catch Amy rolling her eyes in my direction. It was obvious she didn't understand, but since there are only four white people in this class, I was hoping for some support. So sue me.

"*Africana* name. *Puh-leeze!* Ain't nothing African about Natalina," said Judianne, the girl behind me. We used to call her Short Skirt. I know one thing, her clothes fit her better than my name fits me. But try telling her that. "Why don't you just keep the name your mama gave you?" she said.

"Leave the girl alone," said Porscha. "If she wants to change her name, I'm sure she has a reason. People always have reasons for what they do, even if we don't know what they are."

"I know one thing," said Judianne. "She can call herself whatever she wants. It still ain't gonna make her Black." Tanisha shot her a look of disapproval. Judianne lowered her eyes. "Sorry," she said, but it was too late.

I knew someone would misunderstand.

I'm proud to be an Italian. I *love* being Italian. Not that anybody can tell I *am* one, with this blond hair and pale skin of mine.

Everybody else in my family looks typical. Olive complexion, dark hair, dark eyes. Then there's me, sticking out like the proverbial sore thumb. But hey, I might as well. I'm the black sheep, anyway. The only girl in the family who wants a career instead of babies. The only cousin who likes to hang out with Blacks and Latinos. The only one who doesn't think they're all lazy and shiftless. Never mind that they've been discriminated against and shoved to the bottom of the economic rung since they've been here. Try telling that to my father. And don't even mention slavery, he throws his hands up and walks away. So of course he thinks I'm an idiot for wanting to go into social work to help minorities. He might understand better if he knew any.

It's ten years since Dad took over the neighborhood pizza parlor from Uncle Tony. You'd think by now he and my mother would've taken time to get to know most of their customers, not just the white ones. Maybe they're afraid to get too close to someone who might actually hug them, heaven forbid. It seems the only Gamberoni willing to show affection is me. How weird is that?

Some days I wake up wondering if I'm adopted. I try my life on like a dress, and it doesn't fit. I know this life is mine because the label has my name on it, but what kind of name is Sheila? It doesn't tell you who I am, or where I came from. Sheila could be anybody. That's why I wanted something more Africana. Okay, so maybe Africana isn't the right word. But I definitely want something more ethnic. A name that tells a story. A name with roots. That's what I want people to understand.

After English, I met with Mr. Ward and explained all of that, or enough of it to satisfy him, anyway. "Okay," he said. "Then I'll see you tomorrow. Natalina." It was all I could do not to give him a hug.

What's in a Name?

BY NATALINA GAMBERONI

When strangers meet
they hurry past hello and seek
each other's designation.
"My name is——.
And who are you?"
is the spade we sink
into this foreign, hue-man soil
to see what nuggets
we can dig up
what history
what ethnic derivation
what concentration of
cultural genes we can use
to weigh and measure each other.
Some will, no doubt
come up wanting
requiring a change
of designation.

› › ›

"Hello!
My name is Natalina.
Will that do?"

Tyrone

That classroom sounded like a tomb after she read. I'm sitting there studying the video camera, and I'm wondering what Sheila would think if she could hear herself on that tape, if she could watch those words coming out her own mouth.

Judianne's right. There's something wrong with that girl. Hey, lots of peeps change their names, I ain't got no problem with that. Some have to, the names their folks gave them are such dogs. But that girl sound like she wants to change her *race*. What's that about? She feeling guilty 'cause her family's got it good? I don't get it, but I'm gonna leave that one alone.

"Hey, Mr. Ward," I said. "What you planning to do with all them videotapes you're making?"

"I'm going to keep them, maybe show them to my students next year to introduce them to the idea of open-mike readings. If that's okay with you."

"Yeah, that works for me," I said. "Just make sure you show them mine."

Steve Ericson

Sheila may have identity problems, but I don't. I know exactly who I am, and no matter what anybody says, I know I was born in New York City for a reason. Where else does the sidewalk tremble under your feet from the rumble of subways underground, and trucks and city buses up top? Where else do cabbies and garbagemen, bankers and businessmen all walk with a beat? Where else can you find grade A, top of the line characters roaming the streets spouting Shakespeare in the middle of a blizzard? And where else can you find Broadway?

The first time my folks set me down in front of a Broadway stage to watch a musical, and I saw walls rising into the ceiling and staircases disappearing into the floor, I knew: I wanted to be a set designer, and I wanted to work on Broadway.

If you come to my house, there's hardly anywhere to sit in my bedroom, or to step, for that matter, because the whole place is cluttered with hand-painted miniature cardboard sets I designed for imaginary plays. I'll work on real ones as soon as I get to college, because I figure there'll be plenty of opportunities to sharpen my skills working on college productions, especially down at NYU, where I plan to go. If I get in. *When* I get in. I have to get in. I have to get back to the city.

Two months ago, my father announced that we're leaving. We're moving out. The city is getting too rough, he said. Mom's not sure she wants to go on teaching in public schools. She has decided to take a break, so this is a good time to move, he said. As for him, he'll keep his job in publishing and just commute. From *Yorktown Heights*.

I tried to pretend like the move is no big deal, since Mom and Dad are so hot on it, especially Mom, who's been wanting her own house forever. But man, I'm dying. I got friends here that I've grown up and gone to school with all my life, and I fit in here, and you can't tell me there are guys with bleach-blond buzz cuts and earrings in Yorktown. And what about the theater? There's no Broadway in *Yorktown*.

But maybe that's the point. Mom's not too keen on my plans to work in the theater, which is no surprise. She's still trying to get over my wearing an earring, even though I bought the smallest one I could find. (She freaked anyway.) I don't think Dad is too stoked about my plans either, although he doesn't say it because he knows I remember him telling me how he used to want to be an entertainer. He played drums in a band when he was my age, and had big-time plans of hitting the road like Ringo Starr and the Beatles, and doing shows across the country. Then his family moved to Binghamton, away from all his band mates, and eventually, his dream faded away.

Is that why they're moving? Is that what they're hoping happens to me?

Just the thought of maybe never working in the theater makes me crazy, and one day, I tell this story about my father to Raul and I tell him I don't understand how my father's dream could just die like that, when what I really want to know is, can mine. And Raul says something that sticks with me. "Maybe your father's dream wasn't really in his heart. If a dream is in your heart, you never lose it."

After we had that conversation, I kicked my doubts to the back of the closet. (Well, almost. I still go in there now and then.) Part of me continues to be afraid of following in my father's footsteps. These days, though, I try to concentrate on keeping my grades up so I can get into NYU when the time comes, because one thing I know for sure is that my dream is in my heart.

I've got two more years of school to go. Two more years to hold on to my dream, and two more years of Open Mike Fridays. Well, one year and a couple of months—this year's going by so fast. I hope I'll still have a chance to do Open Mike next year. They're so popular now, every kid in school wishes they were in

Mr. Ward's class. I can't blame them. We got a good thing going here, and people need to know about it. We're sick of the negative press teenagers get all the time. Apparently somebody at *The Bronx Insider* agreed. Mr. Ward said they're sending a reporter to cover our next Open Mike Friday, and it should be a monster. Mr. Ward invited a real poet to come speak to us and to read some of his work. It's not an assembly exactly, but Mr. Ward is having us meet together in the multipurpose room for the special presentation. Pedro Pietri is the poet's name. He's in this book called *The United States of Poetry* and somebody said he's a reverend. Sterling must be stoked! Anyway, I'm looking forward to hearing him. Poetry is the coolest thing we got going on in this school now. Maybe I'll still be around next year to enjoy it.

Whether I finish up school here, or in Yorktown Heights depends on my folks. Either way, there's a set designer's job on Broadway with my name on it, and I'm not giving it up for anybody.

Doubtless

BY STEVE ERICSON

When I was seven,
I looked to heaven
and dreamed
of going to the moon
but pretty soon
somebody came along
to change
my tune.
They put me down.
Bang! There my dream lay
on the ground.
Thank God, eventually
I came around
and dreamed
another dream.

At first, it seemed
a good idea to hide it,
confide it
to absolutely no one.

But that was no fun,
besides, I realized
I couldn't. The joy it gave me
just wouldn't
be stopped up. It popped up
at the most
inconvenient times,
effervesced
in all my rhymes.
But, hey! Joy
is not a crime, though
some people
make it seem so.
Does anybody here know
what I mean?
You share your dream
and right away
people laugh,
try to dissuade you,
do what they can to
plant a seed of doubt.
Listen: you've got to
root it out,
laugh last, push past,
pursue. Be you—
whoever that is—
dream intact.
And don't look back.

Don't look back.
Don't look back.
And if you move,
remember: Pack your dreams.
They're portable.

Tyrone

Either that boy's been hanging out with some brothas, or he wish he had. He must've grown up round here, the way he talks. But I hope he ain't studying on hanging out with me. We can peacefully coexist, but I don't have no white boys in my crew.

He ain't half bad, though. Pedro Pietri must've thought so too, the way he clapped when Steve was done. It was kinda cool having a published poet in the audience. First he read to us, then we read to him. He really listened to us too, like we were equals.

I bet Pietri's partly why that reporter came out to our school. Not that the *Insider* is the *Times* or *Daily News*. But hey, it's better than nothing. At least they're interested in the good stuff going on in our neighborhood. Of course, I thought they would send in a brotha, but they sent this white guy. Ain't no telling what kind of piece he'll write about our stuff. Somebody should have told him it's a long way from Shakespeare!

He talked to Rev. Pietri and Mr. Ward, mostly, but

he took notes the whole time we were reading, and his photographer snapped a bunch of pictures. He definitely got one of me. He didn't say which ones they'd be using, though. He got down everybody's name, just in case, so he'd have them for the captions. Hope he spells my name right. Be just my luck, I get in the paper for something *good* and they misspell my name.

The paper comes out next week. See if I ain't the first one at the newsstand.

Raynard Patterson

Finish what you start. That's my mother's favorite saying, and she's earned a right to it. She had me when she was a teenager, but that didn't stop her from finishing high school, and she moved more times than Steve could even dream of! Every now and then, when I consider dropping out, I take a good, long look at my mother and think again.

This year certainly gave me plenty of opportunities to practice.

Homework was a nightmare. Essay questions in history *and* English. What are they trying to do, kill me? All those words swirling around the page gave me a headache I'm still trying to get rid of. If only they could give homework a beat and put it on a CD. Now *that* would work for me. Then they'd be speaking my language. Chords. Melodies. Homework in the key of G. Oh, yeah.

Music has always come easier to me than words. My mother says I used to beat out rhythms on my high chair with a spoon. I don't know if the story's true, but she's told it so often, everyone believes it. The one thing I know for certain is that I eat, sleep, and dream music. Man, when I see myself in the future, it's on a bandstand, fingering my alto. I may not be much of a talker, but hey, give me a sax and I'll talk all night long. My cousin Sterling says one day the whole world will hear what I have to say.

Last week, my English class was the world.

It was Open Mike Friday and I'd shown up with my saxophone case in one hand and a folded-up poem in the other. Not that I needed a copy of the poem. Besides the other kids, I knew we'd have a living, published poet in the audience, so I'd spent a week memorizing and rehearsing my poem in front of a mirror, if you can believe that. Even so, I still thought about maybe skipping the poem and just playing a piece on my sax. But there'd been too much skipping this year for me already. I'd skipped participating in every other Open Mike Friday, and Mr. Ward had skipped over me in class whenever it was time to read aloud. Which is why everybody thought I was three degrees below a moron. Not that I blame them. Even I used to think I was an idiot. Of course, now I know better. So does my English teacher.

Mr. Ward and I had discussed my problem back in September. He'd agreed to keep my secret, although he thought I should share it with the class. As for me, I didn't think they'd understand, and I didn't want anybody treating me as if I was diseased or mentally ill. It seemed easier to let them think I was stupid, so long as I knew I wasn't. But after last Friday, I realized Mr. Ward was right. It's only been a week and already I feel lighter. That's not the way I felt when he called my name, though.

"Okay, Raynard," he said. "You're on."

All my second thoughts rushed forward, causing a traffic jam in my mind. But Gloria caught my eye. "Go on," she whispered. "Do it, Cuz," said Sterling. "Yeah," said Wesley. "Show us what you got."

I nodded thanks and took a deep breath. I shoved the poem in my pocket, grabbed my sax, and went to the front of the room.

Dyslexia

BY RAYNARD PATTERSON

Onion skin, acid-free linen,
80% recycled fiber—
the paper content
doesn't much matter.
My eyes see
letters dancing backward
across whatever page
they're printed on.
The why is a mystery to me.
Could it be I'm one gigabyte short?
Or maybe I was born feet first?
When the doctor smacked my bottom
did I laugh instead of cry?
Do my thoughts trade places
like letters, on the sly?
Such questions are enough
to make you crazy if
you're not.
"Dyslexia is a minor disturbance,
nothing major once you learn
your way around it," says the doc

as if he's a radio jock
announcing a fender-bender.
Steer clear of the wreck ahead.
Try the Triborough
for smoother traffic the next time
you take your mind
for a spin.
Neurological distinction
notwithstanding,
something in me whispers Freak
every time I wriggle out
of reading aloud,
or have to ask a stranger
"Excuse me, but
what does that sign say?"
Read me any way you choose.
Only please, stop asking
"What's his *problem?"*

Tyrone

The world ain't but one big surprise after another. Just look at Raynard. Or look at *Steve.* That white boy got more up his sleeve than anyone would guess. I ain't lying.

Yesterday me, Wesley, and Sterling got up to do a cipher for Open Mike Friday and here come Steve, jumping up to join us. I laughed out loud. Didn't even try to hide it. I ain't never seen no white boy do no free-style poem. You know how hard that is? One person starts a poem, then the next guy has to step into the rhythm, pick up the poem where the first guy left off, and keep it going. Then, after a while, the third guy steps in, if there is a third guy, and he takes over, and then the fourth guy, and so on. You go round and round and round like that, long as you can keep it tight, or until somebody finishes off the poem, or you get tired. Whatever.

Me and Wesley usually team up, going back and forth, with Sterling on guitar layin' down the beat. Sometimes we let Chankara jump in. She ain't half bad either, but then, she's a sister. What you expect? But Steve? Please. So of course I laughed.

"Boy," I said. "Sit your white butt back down before you hurt yo'self."

"Give the guy some slack," said Sterling. See why we call him Preacher?

"Yeah, brother," said Steve.

"You hear this white boy?" I said. I'm thinking he must like to take his life in his hands.

Wesley studied Steve a minute. "The question is, do you flow?" I figured that would be the end of it, 'cause I was sure Steve wouldn't even know what the brotha was talking about. How could he?

"Yeah," said Steve. "I flow."

"Guys?" said Mr. Ward. "Today?"

I shook my head. "Yeah, okay, Teach." I cut my eyes at Steve, betting this boy had never done a cipher in his life.

"Just try to keep up," I told him. "Y'all ready?"

Preacher set up the beat, and we took off.

And guess what? That white boy can *flow*. Makes you kinda wonder 'bout his family tree, now don't it?

What else can that boy do that I don't know about?

News at Five

BY TYRONE BITTINGS,
STEVE ERICSON, AND
WESLEY "BAD BOY" BOONE

There be people in this land who want to take me out
But I will not leave the planet earth without a shout.
You may think you know me well, but let me set you
    straight.
Let me strip away the lies before it gets too late.
News at Five has got you thinking I was born to steal.
Blacks are menacing, they say, as if their talk's for real.
Brothas packing 45s work hard to prove them right.
Thanks to them, nobody's granny can go out at night.
But if Five-O checks my pocket, they will find no piece.
I'm a rapper, not a shooter. Words are my release.
I believe in Martin's power, though the King is gone.
But the last I heard, "I Have a Dream" keeps living on.
So will I, because no matter what the papers say,
I will hold on to tomorrow. I am here to stay.

I am here to stay, yo. I am here to play, yo.

Well, the ball is in my court, because I've come to play.
I am Steve, although they call me Dough Boy every day.
I will not apologize because my eyes are blue.
I am cool with being me just like you're cool with you.
By the way, just 'cause you brothers put the H in hip
doesn't mean some of us white boys can't pick up a tip.
I can get down on the get-down. I know how to flow.
I be checking out Dr. Dre too, if you must know.
But enough of that, 'cause I've got something on my mind.
I have seen the News at Five and here is what I find:
There ain't nothing good on teens, don't matter where you
    look.
Black or white, screen time is strictly for the teenage crook.
Hear them tell it, drugs and violence is our only song.
For myself, I think it's time that we all prove them wrong.

I am here to stay, yo. I am here to play, yo.

Now it's my turn 'cause you always save the best for last.
Mr. Ward just eyed the clock. I better make this fast.
Listen up, my peeps, because I've got the 411.
News at Five is infotainment. That's the game they run.
So forget about those gray heads with their slanted views.
Come tomorrow, we will be the ones to write the news.
Starting now, we can create ourselves a whole new crew.
We can't do no worse than Nixon, I don't think. Do you?
I am not a politician, but I know what's right.
It's high time we knocked the wall down between Black and
    white.

So what's say we end this thing with Steven and Tyrone shaking hands and sharing hugs. Let's leave these two alone!

I am here to stay, yo. I am here to play, yo.

Peace.

Sheila

If anybody had to catch me, I guess I'm glad it was Wesley.

I was in the doorway of a classroom watching Porscha as she walked by. No. That's not right. I wasn't watching Porscha, I was watching the way she *walked,* trying to study it. Then, once she turned the corner, I stepped into the hall and walked just like her. That's when Wesley caught me.

"Girl, what is your problem?"

That's the same question my mother and father keep asking me, although they don't use the exact same words. "What's wrong with you? Why can't you be like your sisters?" I want to know that too. Why *can't* I be like them, be like *somebody*? I hate sticking out.

Everybody around me is dark and ethnic. Which is in, by the way. Look at all the supermodels. They're from places like Venezuela and Africa and Puerto Rico. Then there's me, white bread and pale as the moon. I can't even tan without burning myself. I look around my neighborhood and this school, and nobody looks like me. I keep thinking if I could just stick out *less,* if I could learn to walk and talk like the kids around me, maybe I would fit in more. I don't know. Maybe it's a dumb idea. Wesley sure thinks so. When he pulled me aside in the school hall and I tried to explain why I was copying Porscha's walk, stupid was the word he used. The minute he said it, I felt my cheeks go red. That's not the color I was after. I jerked away from Wesley and avoided his eyes.

"Okay, maybe it was stupid. But I just want to fit in. I'm tired of being different, all right?" Suddenly I thought, Why am I trying to explain this to Wesley? He's Black. He already fits in. "Forget it," I said, beginning to walk away. "You don't understand."

"Oh, get a clue, girl! Everybody's different. It don't matter what your skin color is, or what name you call yourself. Everybody is different inside, anyway. We're all trying to fit in. Ain't nothing new about that."

"Great!" I said. "Since you're so smart, tell me what I'm supposed to do!"

Wesley shrugged. "Hey, I don't know what to tell you, except be yourself."

"Wonderful! Pearls of wisdom. Thanks a lot."

Wesley put his hand on my shoulder. "Sheila," he

said, "you want to hang with brothas and sistas, it ain't no big thing. Just don't try to *be* them. Keep your name, change it—whatever. A name is a personal thing and I'm not going to get into that. But why you want to change who you are? Soon as you get out of here, you're going to go to a college or get a job where everybody else is as blond and blue-eyed as you. They walk like you and talk like you. What're you going to do, then? Change yourself back?"

The truth of his words pinned me to the wall. I never even stopped to think about the future, about leaving this school, this neighborhood, maybe even this city. All I ever think about is now, because now hurts so bad.

"I guess you're right," I said.

"Yeah, well." A couple of sisters passed by and threw us a dirty look. Wesley dropped his hand from my shoulder and shifted from one foot to another, suddenly uncomfortable.

"Look, at least in Mr. Ward's class, we make it easy. You want to hang, you want to fit in? It ain't no big secret. Just bring your poetry every Open Mike Friday and share right along with the rest of us. It's that simple."

"Yeah, I guess I can do that. I did it that one time."

"Yes, you did. Hey, I'm out of here," said Wesley. He jogged down the hall to his next class before I could thank him. Halfway there, he turned back and yelled, "By the way, forget Porscha's walk. It ain't working for you."

I don't know where it came from, but somewhere inside myself, I found a smile.

Private Puzzle

BY SHEILA GAMBERONI

God must love puzzles
the way he scatters our pieces
across the table of the world.
Here, squares bathed in shadow
appear to be the same
though each bears a different name.
It's only on closer examination
I learn that no two pieces
are alike.
Is that the plan?
To force confrontation?
Investigation?
Communication?
I raise my hand to ask
but am told
to move along.
So I nudge through the crowd,
scrape my shins,
feel the crush of bone,
moan a little,
then cry loud enough

for anyone to hear.
But still I go on seeking
an angular slot
to slip myself into,
someplace that feels
like home.
A friend points me
to the podium.
There!
For a moment,
the puzzle is done.
We are one now—
Eighteen syllables.
A single poem.

Tyrone

That girl's threatening to be a regular feature. This is the second week in a row she's brought something to read for Open Mike Friday. Except for me and Wesley, I don't think anybody's read two times in a row. But hey, she can read all she wants. Least she ain't talking that Africana mess no more. Good thing too. Now even Judianne can stand to have her in the same room.

If that girl ain't careful, somebody might actually end up liking her.

Janelle

Jojo asked me to marry him yesterday. When Tyrone heard me telling Lupe that, he laughed his head off.

Jojo is eight years old. He's one of the kids I tutor at the public library. I was there yesterday helping him prepare for a math test when he suddenly cocked his head, looked up at me and said, "Miss Janelle, you're the most beautifulest lady on this whole planet."

"Thanks, Jojo."

"I been thinkin', Miss Janelle. Maybe we should get married."

Just like that! Out of the blue. Jojo sounded so serious, it was hard not to laugh. I didn't want to hurt his feelings though, so I pretended to cough a couple of times and covered my face.

"Well! I'll have to think about that," I said. "But first, we have to get you into the fourth grade. Deal?"

"Deal," he said. Jojo's such a cutie.

I'm glad somebody finds me beautiful, even if he is

just eight years old! But maybe he's not the only one, though. Not anymore. The kids in Mr. Ward's class sure look at me differently these days. I noticed that at the last Open Mike Friday.

When I first got up to read, I was my usual self. I sucked in my stomach, walked slow to make sure nothing jiggled, and tugged down on my shirt, like I could really hide my extra pounds under there. I waited for Mr. Ward to switch on the video and then started to read.

I looked up from the page a few times and noticed kids in the front row with their eyes closed, smiling. Amy and Tanisha nodded every now and then, like I'd said something familiar, something they understood. Judianne, Leslie, and Porscha leaned forward so they could hear every word. Everybody really listened to what I had to say, even the guys. Tyrone, Wesley, Steve, Raul, Devon—they all stared at me like I was someone special. And nobody cared about the size of my body. Not even me.

The Door

BY JANELLE BATTLE

I've been busy lately
carving a door of words
without a lock in sight.
Your ear is the key
that lets you into me.

(I am a secret
I want to share.
I swing my door open
and say a prayer.)

Look around.
Take the tour.
Fear hangs on the wall
and shame, sometimes.
Emotional dislocation too.
But I am brave
in my admission.
Are you?

When no one is looking
I check to see
if anyone else seems
as scared as me,
or lonely, or shy,
or insecure.
Is it just me?
I'm not so sure.

Is your heart
like an onion too?
Show me yours,
I'll show you mine
we used to say.
Your turn.
Peel away.

Tyrone

Janelle made it into the paper. I did too—in the group shot, looking all fuzzy. Devon was the only one got a close-up. They just love them pretty boys. That's okay. I got my name in there.

Mr. Ward brought the paper to school and held it up for the class to see. "Look at this headline," he said. "'Student Poets Bloom in the Bronx.' That's you guys!"

I don't know who was prouder, us or Mr. Ward.

He brought a few extra copies of the paper for the class, and passed them around for anyone who hadn't seen it. I'd already bought my own, though. I had to, 'specially since they quoted what I said about how our poetry gives us a release, how it helps us relate to one another. They said our stuff was "energetic" and "rich in positive social messages." My moms will frame this puppy, for sure.

I called the reporter this afternoon and thanked him for writing such a nice piece. I told him about our assembly. "We'll be jamming," I told him. "Why don't you come check us out?" He said he'd try to make it.

Maybe we can get us another write-up out of this. You never know.

Lupe

I went to Janelle's this afternoon to study. Of course, before we could get started, she wanted to dish about Raul. Him and me had our first date over the weekend and, as far as Janelle's concerned, it's the biggest news since we all had our pictures splashed across the local paper. I know she's been dying to find out what happened. She called me twice, but I was at the library. She left a message asking if we planned on doing a love poem duet for assembly in a few weeks. That girl's crazy! I am looking forward to our last Open Mike Friday, though.

"So. You finally went out with him," said Janelle.

"Yeah."

"Well?"

"Well what?" I bite my tongue to keep from laughing. I know this is killing her.

"What did you and Latin Loverboy do?"

"We went to a movie."

"And?"

"And what? We watched it and he took me home."

"And?"

"And *nothing*. Now, can we please get to work?"

"Girl, you are no fun anymore. All you want to do is work, work, work."

"Yeah, well, fun ain't going to get me through history or trig."

Janelle stuck her tongue out at me and cracked open her history book, looking all disappointed. I balled up a piece of paper and threw it at her. She looked up, surprised, and threw it back, laughing. Then we settled down.

It's great having somebody to study with, even though I do okay on my own. Mr. Ward says if I keep pulling up all my other grades the way I've pulled up my grade in English, I should be able to get into a decent college when I graduate. That's what I'm planning on.

I want to go somewhere out of state, somewhere away from home, away from Berto and his drinking buddies. I'll miss my sister, Christina, and her little Rosa, though. But I don't see them as much as I used to, anyway. I'm too busy with school.

I'm not sure what I want to major in at college. I know I want to do something with kids, though. Maybe become a kindergarten teacher, or a pediatrician. Gloria says I still got time to figure that out. Keeping my grades up so I can get into a good school—that's the main thing.

Christina says I'm the smart one. "I envy you,

Lupe," she told me last night. I could hardly believe my ears. "I wish I had gone to college," she said.

Getting to college takes more than wishing, I can tell you that much.

I've got an exam tomorrow, so I better put in an extra hour of study. I don't know what the questions are going to be, but I want to make sure I'm ready for whatever they throw at me.

imagine

BY LUPE ALGARIN

I walk by a mirror,
catch my eye,
wonder at the universe
behind it.
Past the flashing eyes
is a file
for yesterday's sunset
dripping mango light,
for Papi's laughter
tinkling in my
five-year-old ears
so many years gone by,
for tears
shed below a crucifix
on my wall.
I sort it all out,
store it under
"been there, done that"
and open a clean drawer
labeled Mañana,

a place to store adventures
I'm still learning
to imagine.

Tyrone

Something's different about Lupe's voice. It's still soft, but it's like there's steel running through it now. I don't think I'm making that up. Anyway, I know one thing for sure. I don't catch her staring off the way I used to. She's always looking straight up now, paying attention to whatever the teacher is saying, like she's afraid to miss a word. I see her running off to the library a lot lately too. Something new is definitely up with that girl.

Diondra

It was an accident. I didn't mean to leave them out for my father to find. At least, I don't think I did. That's what I told Lupe when she asked me what was wrong this morning. I was still upset about my father throwing a fit when he found my art school brochures last night. You'd think I'd stabbed him in the heart, the way he looked at me.

I'm sorry he feels so bad, but there's nothing I can do about it. I've made up my mind. If I can get into an art school, I'm going. Mr. Ward thinks I have a good chance of getting a scholarship. We'll see. Mom says my dad will come around. Eventually. I'm not so sure. Before I left home today, I slipped a poem and a drawing of Michael Jordan in my father's easy chair, under the remote. That way, he wouldn't miss them. I was planning to give him the drawing for his birthday, but after seeing those brochures, he looked like he needed a transfusion, so why wait? Maybe a drawing of his hero will make him feel better. Besides, doing basketball portraits is the closest I'll ever get to my father's dreams for me, so I might as well let him enjoy one now.

I hope Mom's right, though. I hope he does come around. I'm just not holding my breath.

Self-Portrait:
A Poem for My Father

BY DIONDRA JORDAN

I've told you this before
but I guess it bears repeating.
Love is not me being
who you want.
Your definition
is a whirlpool
trying to suck me in
and I'm drowning.
Don't you see?
Don't you hear?
I'm gurgling,
battling for air,
wishing you cared about
what matters to me.
But you can't,
or won't.
Either way, I dip into
my imagination,
grab a rail

and pull myself free.
It's time, Dad.
Time you stop telling me
who to be,
how to live.
This is my portrait.
You chose your canvas.
Let me choose mine.

Tyrone

I didn't get her first few poems, but I dig this one.

The future is ours. Let us have it. That's what she's saying. That's what we're all saying. But I'm lucky. These days my moms ain't trying to push me in one direction or another. She's just glad I have one.

I read her this poem I wrote called "Dream" about doing hip-hop with my own band, and she started crying. My moms don't cry easy, so I felt bad. But she said they were happy tears. "You keep writing, baby," she said. "You're doing good."

I love my moms.

Porscha Johnson

I slam my lunch tray down on the table across from Leslie and Chankara. Diondra looks up, startled, from the next table, then turns back to her lasagna.

"The minute I turn twenty-one, I'm changing my name," I say to no one in particular. "I mean it."

"Why wait?" says Chankara. We've had this conversation before. "Why not change it now?"

I shake my head. "Too complicated."

"Fine, then. Count to ten, and try this." She slices off a square of pizza from her plate and shoves it in my mouth.

Chankara's a problem solver. She has no patience for talking a thing to death. Do something about it or shut up is her motto. I guess she's right. But one of these days, the name Porscha will have to go. I'm tired of providing oversized boys with the raw material for adolescent jokes about my being a high-maintenance mama, or some sort of luxury item. Then there are those oily, leering, dirty old men on my block who drool or wink at me when I pass by on my way home, asking if they can take me for a test drive. Please. But for now, I'm stuck with Porscha. I can live with it a while longer, though.

It's amazing how easy it is to get a bad reputation. My whole life, I ran around letting people pick on me, laughing it off when they teased me, fast-talking my way out of fights. They'd call me four eyes, or stuck-up, or Miss Bug-eyed Bookworm, and I'd pretend their words were water and let them roll off of my back. Now, I'm nobody's duck, and their words stung a whole lot more than water, but I held my temper. It took a bully nine straight months of riding me to cause my thermometer to boil. And once I lost it, did anybody blame it on the bully? No. They start calling me crazy, whispering it behind my back. It was as if that other Porscha, the easygoing, even-tempered one, never existed. Truth is, she always did, always will.

Diondra and Chankara know that. And now, so does Leslie. If only the other kids knew the truth. I could never beat anybody the way I beat Charmayne last year. I'd be afraid to. What if I couldn't stop? What if there was no one around to pull me off? I could kill somebody. I know it's in me. I've got Mama's blood running in my veins, haven't I? She came close enough to killing me, more than once.

When I was twelve, she went on one of her tears and punched me from one side of the room to the other because I didn't wash the dishes. I don't think that was the real reason, though. She was probably just stressed out from working overtime, from dealing with a hard-to-please new boss, or from juggling bills, and I caught the hard end of it. But who cares about the real reasons? The thing is, the same kind of ugly anger lives in me. I couldn't really see that until Charmayne brought it out. I have to make sure that monster never shows her face again, no matter what.

So I find ways to keep her in check. When anger rips a hole in me now, I punch a wall, or run 'til the wind cuts my breath off. Once, I sat on a curb running a piece of broken bottle across my fingertips. Lucky for me the shard had a dull edge that left a jigsaw of scratches on me, but not a whole lot of blood. I know it was a stupid thing to do, but anything's better than allowing those fingers to hurt somebody else. I couldn't live with that. Not again. Not ever.

No, these kids have nothing to fear from me. They just don't know it.

Leslie says I've got to learn to let people in, and I know she's right. Poetry just may be a way to do that. I mean, it worked for Devon, didn't it? And Tyrone. We all got to see another side of them. Even Janelle gets up there—Miss Shyness herself! I've never seen her turn so bold, although the boldness only seems to last as long as she's up front reading her poems. Still, that's something. Tyrone was the biggest surprise, though. Who would have guessed he wrote poetry? And he knows his poems by heart, no less.

Every Friday there he is, the first one to raise his hand when Mr. Ward asks who's got something they want to read. And he's always the first one up, if Mr. Ward gives him the chance. No goofing around like he usually does either. He's all business. He takes center stage, clears his throat, and smoothly launches into his rhyme.

The first time he got up there, I rolled my eyes like half the sisters in class, certain he was going to spout something lame or nasty about girls and sex, or gangsters. I mean, that's all we ever heard him talk about, right? But there was nothing lame about this poem, and none of it was about sex. It was about what's going on in the world, and about trying to make sense of it. It was a poem by somebody who really thinks about things, and that somebody turned out to be Tyrone. He made me change my mind about him that day. Maybe I can change people's minds about me too. It's worth a shot. I better do it quick, though. There are only a few Open Mike Fridays left before school's out, and the last one will be at assembly, and I don't plan on getting up in front of a whole group of strangers my first time out.

Friday is two days away, and I know exactly what poem I'm going to read.

A Letter to My Mother

BY PORSCHA JOHNSON

Dear Mom,
You with the hypodermic needle in your arm,
I never said good-bye, or joined your funeral procession
because I was too angry at the time.

Leaving me seemed to be your choice.
Why make it? Was it something that I did or said?
Weeks after you were dead, those questions
hammered me until I thought my heart would shatter.

But then, as my friend told me, the why of your absence
doesn't really matter. Besides, I'm older now
and understand a little about pain, and the crazy things
it drives us to. So, even though this may be overdue
(remember: Some things are better late than never)—
Mom, I finally forgive you.

Love,
Porscha.

P.S.
Good-bye.

Tyrone

Now I know school's almost over. We came to our English class yesterday and found our poems and drawings gone from the wall. Porscha was about to freak, along with everybody else, 'til Mr. Ward surprised us with a class anthology. He'd gone to some quick-copy place and made up books for each of us with copies of our work. It was pretty cool the way he hooked it up. I can't wait to show my moms.

It was kinda sad seeing the walls all bare. But hey, today was our last Open Mike Friday, so it was time for our stuff to come down. Besides, we were only in there long enough to take attendance. Then we headed for the auditorium to have Open Mike there as part of assembly, just like Mr. Ward planned.

The hall was crowded by the time I got there. I looked around for that reporter, but I don't think he made it. Yeah, well, I thought. His loss.

I slipped into a seat in the front row just as the principal called everybody to attention. Sitting up front ain't my thing, but this assembly was different.

Our whole class was there so we could reach the stage quicker to read our work. I was down with that.

The principal made a couple of announcements, but don't ask me about what. Nobody was interested. We all sat up, though, when he called Teach to the stage.

Mr. Ward explained what Open Mike Friday was about and how we got started. (Wesley yelling, "Y'all got me to thank! Remember that!") I was only half listening 'cause I was waiting 'til Teach got to the good stuff, meaning when we finally got to read.

"Before we get started," he said, "I thought it would be good if one or two of the students who have participated in Open Mike this year would say a few words about what it has meant to them." I checked down the row real quick.

"I'll pass," said Leslie.

Amy and Sheila had "Don't look at me" stamped all over their faces. Raul didn't look much better.

Sterling rose outta his seat, but then sat back down. Cracked me up. Everybody was suddenly shy. Not me. I stood, headed for the podium.

I cleared my throat, rolled my shoulders a few times to get relaxed.

"Today, Tyrone," said Mr. Ward.

"Yeah, my brotha," chimed in Porscha.

"I'm getting there," I said, taking a second to adjust the microphone. "Hello? Can you hear me?"

"Yeah, fool, but you ain't saying nothing," said Chankara.

"Aiight. Just give me a minute." Everybody laughed.

"Okay. I just wanted to say I'm really glad I got to do this poetry thing because I feel like, even though the people in our class are all different colors and some of you speak a different language and everything, I feel like we connected. I feel like I know you now. You know what I'm saying? I feel like we're not as different as I thought."

I looked out at Raul, Janelle, Gloria, Devon, my homey Wesley—my whole crew—and felt something deep inside my chest, something that made me swallow hard.

"You guys are okay," I said. "Even you, Steve, with your skinny, bleach-blond self." Steve grinned. Raynard patted him on the back and everybody else tee-heed for a hot second. Then I went back to my seat.

When I sat down, our whole crew was clapping. Tanisha and Judianne whistled. Nobody said it, but it was like I had spoken for all of us. You know what I'm saying? And that don't happen every day.

I'm glad I didn't choke up there, 'cause now the whole school's talking about that assembly. Probably be talking about it all summer, we was so hot. We sizzled! Chankara read, Raul did his Zorro thing, my man Wesley and me did a new cipher with a little sax from Raynard, and I even got Porscha to read her piece again. I never did come up with any African drum music for Tanisha, but the sista did fine all by herself.

Except for Wesley and me, we all pretty much did our old poems. The kids in our class were the only ones who'd already heard them. Besides, most of the kids want to wait 'til next year to break out the new stuff, 'cause Mr. Ward already told us he plans to have Open Mike in all his classes then. Cool, huh?

After assembly, Mr. Ward came up and clapped me on the back. "I like what you had to say, Tyrone. And I loved your cipher," he told me. "Any chance I'll see you next year?"

"I don't know, Mr. Ward," I said. "I've been thinking about hooking up with some guys who want to start a band. I might have to skip school and go on tour, you know what I'm saying? So I can't make no promises." I'm blowing smoke about this tour and Teach knows it, but that's the game.

"I understand. But I did want to let you know, we'll be hosting a poetry slam here next year," said Mr. Ward.

And guess what. All of a sudden, the man's got my attention.

Epilogue

My mother says I'm lucky. She thinks I should be thrilled to go to an American school every day. I pretend I'm happy, for her sake. She doesn't understand what it's like for me. Nobody does.

My name is Mai Tren. I'm half Black, half Vietnamese. You try being me for a week, see how well you fit into this world. "Go back where you came from," kids say to me sometimes. And I think, Go where exactly? We left the village my mother grew up in many years ago, right after my father died. He was American, so my mother was able to bring our family to the United States. I have as much right to be here as anyone. But no one hears me. No one cares about that. They can't see past my slanted eyes. Not even the Black kids. Never mind that we're all people of color, that most of us live in single-parent homes, that we catch the same amount of grief from the white world. It's ridiculous.

I'll be all right, though. I'll finish high school, go to college, get my law degree, and be out of here. I just can't count on having too many friends along the way.

Black people keep reminding me that I'm not one of them. Asians shun me because my blood is not "pure." And whites are still making up their minds, although some want me to be their friend so I can help them with their math! Which is a joke, because I don't like math. So where does that leave me? I look around this class, with Black kids, Latinos, Jews, and Italians, and I wonder how I'm ever supposed to connect with any of them.

But then we had an assembly yesterday with all these kids reading poetry. They seemed to get along with each other, almost like a family. They said it was the poems that brought them together. It can't be that simple, can it?

Their teacher is supposed to be doing poetry again next year. Maybe I'll get his class. Who knows? I can think of worse things.